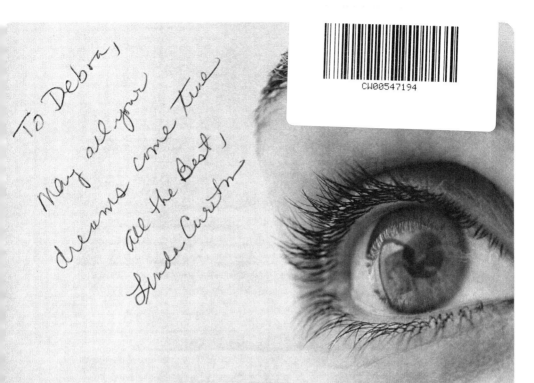

THE LEADERSHIP
MUSE

Inspiration for the 21st Century Hero-Leader

LINDA Y. CURETON

synergy
press

Synergy Press books may be purchased in bulk for educational, business,
or sales promotional use. For information please write:
order@synergypressonline.com

FIRST EDITION

Designed by Jennifer Tyson

Library of Congress Cataloging-in-Publishing Data

Cureton, Linda Y.
    The Leadership Muse
Leadership, self-help / Linda Y. Cureton. – 1st ed.
        p. cm.
    Includes references.
    ISBN: 978-0-9802209-6-4
1. Cureton, Linda Y., date.
2. Women-United States-Biography
3. Leadership

dedication

To Mama from Toot

table of contents

part one
Invoking the Tenth Muse of Leadership

chapter 1

Silver gray hair
Neatly combed in place
There were four generations
Of love on her face
She was so wise
No surprise passed her eyes
She's seen it all

EXCERPT FROM THE SONG BETTER DAYS BY DIANNE REEVES

My career path has led me to a C-level executive position, one in which I am charged with inspiring an organization where rocket science is the order of the day. My calling is to innovate and advance information technology so that the explorers, scientists, and engineers may occupy their thoughts with reaching for the stars. I serve people whose mission is to plumb the depths of the known universe. So if anyone needs a Muse – some divine stroke of inspiration from sources unknown – it is me.

In January of 2010, while pondering my New Year's resolutions, I first encountered what I now know to be the "Leadership Muse." My resolutions usually reflect a desire to lead effectively, with authority and grace. I reflect on questions many leaders ask themselves: *What does it take to be a good leader? Where do you learn "leadership"? To whom can leaders turn for knowledge? Or for inspiration?*

But on this particular day, my musings were cut short. My grandmother, Corona, better known as Mama by her family and friends, was celebrating her 96th birthday, and the whole family was gathering for a traditional feast. I made her favorite Sweet Potato Crescent Rolls and "Baptist" Pound Cake. The evening was all about family, fried chicken, and macaroni and cheese. I would think more about leadership, learning, innovation, and resolutions later. We had a wonderful birthday dinner for Mama. At the end of the evening, I kissed her goodnight, and she died the next morning.

In the midst of the whirlwind of emotions I experienced after she passed away, my resolutions were transformed into a new vision of leadership for the 21st century – a vision inspired by a woman whose lifetime spanned nearly a century and who had seen technology advance faster than the speed of light. As I thought about my grandmother, her life, and what she meant to me, I realized that the answers to my questions about leadership, knowledge, and inspiration were all around me. In fact, Mama taught me much about what it takes to lead – for example, that great leaders must be good communicators, visionaries, and creative problem solvers. They must also be courageous, caring, and authentic.

Many excellent books have been written enumerating the qualities and skills necessary for good leadership, but Mama *lived* it. Books tell how to lead. Mama *showed* what it is to lead, and she is a fitting study with which to begin these a-musing leadership lessons.

LEADERS ARE GREAT COMMUNICATORS. Mama was an expert communicator who didn't let language barriers get in her way. My grandfather served in the Army as a dentist and traveled extensively with my grandmother until he retired as a colonel in 1976. During his tenure with the Army, they were stationed in Germany twice, so Mama learned German. She was also fluent in sign language. My sisters and I used to joke that

Also available from W. W. Norton & Co., Inc.

New York & London

The Body Remembers Casebook:

Unifying Methods and Models in the Treatment of Trauma and PTSD

by Babette Rothschild

A companion to *The Body Remembers*, *The Body Remembers Casebook*, contains an assortment of complex cases presented in a variety of writing styles: case reports, session-by-session narratives, single session transcripts. Each case is approached with a combination of methods ranging from traditional psychodynamic approaches and applications of attachment theory to the most innovative trauma methods.

Treatment methods used include: body psychotherapy, cognitive behavioral therapy, eye movement desensitization and reprocessing, Gestalt therapy, neuro-linguistic programming, the SIBAM model of Levine, somatic trauma therapy, and transactional analysis.

"*The Body Remembers Casework* is a treasure trove of wisdom, integration, and common sense." — David Grand, Ph.D., author of *Emotional Healing at Warp Speed* and *The Power of EMDR*, developer of The Grand System of creativity/performance/healing enhancement

The Body Remembers Casebook

$19.95 USA • ISBN 0-393-70400-9 (pbk) • 7 1/8" x 10" • 224 pages

Order by phone: 800-233-4830 or fax 800-458-6515
Order by email: mcerminaro@wwnorton.com
Order via Internet: www.wwnorton.com/psych

Also available from W. W. Norton & Co., Inc.

New York & London

Help for the Helper:

The Psychophysiology of Compassion Fatigue and Vicarious Trauma

by Babette Rothschild

"Help for the Helper, so clearly written and well organized, will benefit any practitioner who wants to avoid the fatigue that interferes with treatment of the people who are most in need of our help." — Marion F. Solomon

Therapist burnout is a pressing issue. Self-care and risk-avoidance are possible only when therapists actively help themselves. The difference in the new awareness that Rothschild recommends will be felt not just in the life and well-being of the therapist, but also in the therapy hour as this attentiveness has its affect on the exchange between therapist and client.

Contents in Detail: Preface: Using Common Sense • Introduction: *Overview; Organization; Disclaimer* • 1. Psychotherapists at Risk: *Therapist Assets and Deficits; Identifying Terminology; Countertransference; Projective Identification; Empathy* • 2. Managing the Ties That Bind: *Theory—The Neurophysiology of Empathy; Somatic Empathy; Mirroring and Mimicry; Skill Building—Facial and Postural Awareness; Conscious Postural Mirroring; Unmirroring* • 3. Keeping Calm: *Theory—The Neurophysiology of Arousal; Skill Building—Arousal Awareness: The Therapist's Brakes; How Close is Too Close?; Controlling Empathic Imagery* • 4. Thinking Clearly: *Theory—The Neurophysiology of Clear Thinking; Skill Building—Know Thyself; Strengthening the Observer; Controlling Self-Talk; Nurturing Your Work Space; Structured Self-Care* • 5. Concluding Reflections: *Revisiting Projective Identification; To Each Her Own Chair; Final Words* • Appendices: *Assessment; Pilot Research*

Help for the Helper

$32.00 USA • ISBN 0-393-70422-X • 6-1/8" x 9-1/4" • 256 pages

Order by phone: 800-233-4830 or fax 800-458-6515
Order by email: mcerminaro@wwnorton.com
Order via Internet: www.wwnorton.com/psych

Mama didn't let the fact that you couldn't hear her stop her from talking! A masterful conversationalist, she rose above most communication barriers.

Likewise, great leaders speak to people in their own languages. As a technologist and an IT leader, I must be able to speak the language of information technology (IT) *and* the language of business, depending on my audience. In the past, I might have said to a business leader, "We need an enterprise architecture that defines business and technical reference models which map the as-is state of our infrastructure and create an IT capital plan mapping out our to-be state." And I would be met with slack-jawed, dumb-founded stares. Thankfully, my grandmother taught me how to translate quickly, without losing a beat. In "Mama-speak," I transform the previous sentence to: "We need to know where we are, where we are going, why we want to go there, and how we plan to make it happen." Suddenly, their expressions change to reflect understanding and interest, and I can proceed to demonstrate how IT can help us get the information we need to move forward.

LEADERS HAVE COURAGE. Mama was very brave. I saw her go up against a pit bull with just a broom and a water hose … and win. I was with her as she sped around Fort George G. Meade in my grandfather's red Alpha Romeo convertible. She got pulled over by the military police … but still won. While in Germany, Mama was a minority in a foreign country, yet became president of the Officer's Wives Club – a first.

I found an old picture of Mama sitting with three other officers' wives. She seemed somewhat out of place, yet held her head high and gracefully, sporting handmade, lace gloves and just a tad more lipstick than a typical 1960s woman would wear. I could see fear in her eyes, but most of all, I could see courage and hesitant dignity on her pursed lips. Mama certainly felt both emotions, but courage won out. After all, what is courage if not learning to manage and *despite* fear? Without fear, there is no need for courage. Her fear inspired her courage, and her courage inspired me.

MAMA (FAR LEFT) WITH OFFICER'S WIVES CLUB (CIRCA 1968).

LEADERS ARE INNOVATIVE. They must be creative, versatile, resourceful, and resilient, because they will face unprecedented challenges throughout their careers that will force them to use these talents. Mama could crochet, knit, sew, and do needlepoint. She taught me, a lefty, how to crochet left-handed and knit right-handed, and how to use a pair of right-handed pinking shears. She could also do ceramics, masonry, and plumbing. She could hang dry-wall or plaster walls, repair shoes, perform basic masonry work, and fix a car. She could heal any "boo-boo," and I still believe that she could have done minor surgery if necessary. My sister, Lisa, and I cleaned out her closet and found a pair of spike-heeled, patent-leather shoes and a battlefield dental-repair kit. We knew these two things were somehow related, but we couldn't quite figure out how … except that Mama knew exactly what to do with both.

My grandmother was, and continues to be, my inspiration. But this isn't a book about my grandmother, nor is it a book about being a CIO. This is a book about the inspirational leadership lessons waiting to reveal themselves in every area of our lives – if we would only open our eyes to the Muses disguised as everyday moments and ordinary people.

Odysseus had Athena, Superman had Lois, and John Smith had Pocahontas. These women (or goddesses, in one case) were Muses who inspired their heroes to do the impossible, the divine, and the magical. They inspired their heroes to communicate flawlessly and rallied courage and innovation in these men, even when they were ready to give up. Likewise, there is a Leadership Muse flirting just outside the pages of this book. I'm hoping my pen will lure her in so that she can inspire any modest reader who secretly wants to be a hero too.

As leaders, each of us must seek and find our own Muses – those people or lessons that inspire us to do the difficult, heroic things. Inspiration parades around as clear as day, but unless you are careful, you might not recognize your Muse. She might be disguised as your grandmother, your father, an old television show, music, nature, or even your hairdresser. So listen carefully, lest you miss the moment she reveals herself.

I will now call forth the Muse of Writing to help me record the words, phrases, sentences, and paragraphs that faithfully represent the wonder of epic leadership.

Sweet Muse, come in my heart.
With truth and love, I start.
My vision, my insight,
My wisdom ignites.
Urging, cheering, prompting,
Trying and inspiring —
God's messenger divine,
An angel for all time.
No, Lord, I won't refuse.
I'm thankful for your Muse.

"INVOCATION OF THE MUSE"
BY LINDA Y. CURETON, 2011

chapter 2

"[M]adness comes from the Muses. This takes hold
upon a gentle and pure soul, arouses it and inspires it ...
But he who without the divine madness comes to the doors of the
Muses, believing that technique alone will make him a good poet,
he and his sane compositions never reach perfection, but are utterly
eclipsed by the performances of the inspired madman."

PLATO IN PHAEDRUS

At the end of my first semester of college, I was low on cash, so I applied for a temporary position working during the Christmas season at Sears. I assumed retail work would be fairly easy ... until I learned what the job entailed. I would have to offer live demonstrations of drill guides – attachments that fit on drills to help ensure accuracy – and would receive commission for each one sold during my shift.

Sadly, woodworking was one vocation my grandmother didn't think to prepare me for; I knew nothing about drills or tools. And to make matters more challenging, I was a very shy, quiet 17 year old who preferred blending into the background, unless I was hiding behind a French horn. This was going to be a difficult job for me to get and perform – but the pay was good, and my desire for some spending money outweighed my stage fright.

Dozens of hopeful salespeople were instructed on how to use the drill guides and given a script. Though I had never used a drill, I discovered it wasn't too much harder than using Mama's right-handed pinking shears. After the training, the deciding moment came – the "audition." There were only three sales positions. I decided I would have to act crazy – or at least my version of it – if I was going to get one of them. With a voice I hadn't even suspected could come out of me, I shrugged off my usual shy personality and made my sales pitch a crazed theatrical performance – singing the script and inspiring every person within earshot to "drill accurate and perfect holes EVERY time for only $19.99!" And I got the job.

Afterwards, the perplexed trainer asked me how a person who seemed so shy and quiet could pull that off. I shrugged and laughed, pretending not to know what came over me, but the truth was that I simply acted crazy. And I sold a lot of drill guides that holiday season. Just a little touch of madness was all it took to catapult my performance out of mediocrity and into the realm of inspiration. Years later, when I came across the words of the ancient Greeks describing the madness of the Muses, I realized that perhaps my intuition to "act crazy" that day had been inspiration from my Muse.

In Plato's *Phaedrus*, a dialogue on love and writing, the philosopher Socrates explains different forms of insanity, zeroing in on divine madness. Love is a divine madness, and so is creative imagination. "Madness, provided it comes as the gift from heaven, is the channel by which we receive the greatest blessings," says Socrates.

In Socrates' time, people believed the nine original Muses brought divine madness to those they favored, transforming ordinary men and women into first-rate artists and geniuses. The Muses – daughters of Mnemosyne, goddess of memory, and Zeus, king of the gods – were immortal. Each goddess had her chosen art, including: poetry (epic, love, and lyric), history, tragedy, music, dance, comedy, and astronomy. And when she would observe a special devotee of her favorite discipline – an astronomer gazing into other galaxies and pondering the origins of the universe and the very first light, a poet spinning threads of rhyme into tapestries of reality by the glow of a single candle, or a painter striving to represent truth and reality with the precise strokes of his brush – the Muse would descend from heaven and bestow upon him the gift of divine madness required for inspired creativity and problem solving.

As human innovation creates more and more avenues of expression, it's only natural that the nine original Muses have given birth to a host of children – Muses for our modern arts. One can imagine a Muse of Mechanics taking shape during the industrial revolution, and perhaps a Muse of Technology guiding Robert Goddard's hand as he developed the rocket. These days, the ethereal Muse of Social Networking works her magic in everyday exchanges between people and communities.

Surely, throughout time and for times such as these, there exists a Leadership Muse to inspire those who burn the candle at both ends, who endure long nights and intense pressure while leading people through change, uncertainty, tough times, and difficult challenges. Inspired and lasting leadership requires that touch of divine madness that the Muses bestow upon their devotees. In fact, most of history's greatest leaders were at least a little crazy. In his book, *A First-Rate Madness: Uncovering the Links Between Leadership and Mental Illness,* author Nassir Ghaemi suggests that during times of crisis, we are "much better off being led by mentally-ill leaders than by mentally-normal ones." Martin Luther King, Jr., Mahatmas Gandhi, and other world-changing leaders exhibited resilience, realism, empathy, and creativity. These qualities, Ghaemi suggests, are a result of their suffering from mania and depression. Seeing and understanding all the injustices and hardships in the world may have taken them to some dark and twisted places, but it also inspired them to change things, to bring about the unimaginable but beautiful realities they envisioned – and gave them the courage to do it.

Today's leadership crisis often demands the ability to embrace two very different extremes – risk-taking and foresight, empathy and justice, optimism and pragmatism. We need leaders with a little *crazy* in them to help us navigate today's organizational challenges – and to inspire those who follow them to do the "impossible." Leaders who cannot embrace an inner edge are what Ghaemi refers to as non-crisis leaders. The so-called *normal* leader is commonplace and seeks to conform and preserve her past. She will see problems and challenges and make busy work of doing nothing. She will solve the easy problems and do very little to learn and grow. Unaffected by the madness of a leadership muse, this leader will not connect to others and will rarely overcome adversity.

Luke Skywalker, from the *Star Wars* movies, possesses many of the traits of Ghaemi's crisis leader. His destiny calls him to shed the pain of a fatherless childhood and save his people from the oppression and tyranny of the Dark Side. Luke finds his inner edge as he battles his past and his hatred. Yoda cautions Luke about the importance of winning this battle. "Fear is the path to the dark side," he says. "Fear leads to anger. Anger leads to hate. Hate leads to suffering."

In *Star Wars V: The Empire Strikes Back*, Yoda trains Luke to make his mind do the impossible. Though Luke can telekinetically move rocks while standing on his head, he finds the task of moving a spacecraft more daunting. When Yoda encourages him to do it, Luke says that he will "try." Yoda admonishes him: "No. Try not. Do or do not. There is no try." Normal leaders try; crazy leaders *do*.

Crazy (or *inspired*) leaders understand and live by Yoda's maxims. They embrace challenges, seek new solutions, and accomplish what most people cannot. And touched by a little of the Muse's divine madness, they convince others that they, too, can achieve the impossible, the divine, and the magical.

chapter 3

THE BREATH OF INSPIRED LEADERSHIP

"To lead requires those who willingly follow.
It requires those who believe in something bigger than
a single issue. To inspire starts with the clarity of WHY."

SIMON SINEK
AUTHOR OF **START WITH WHY: HOW GREAT LEADERS**
INSPIRE EVERYONE TO TAKE ACTION

Call me crazy, but I believe in the Leadership Muse. She is not just a product of my delusional mind or an object of literary convenience. She does her work in C-suites all over the world, and her results are tangible. Look for her influence in the presence of the greatest leaders. She leaves her mark.

Just as the Muse exists to inspire leaders, leaders exist to inspire as well, perhaps even to serve as Muses for others. Eighty-six percent of people believe that the ability to inspire people is a critical leadership trait, according to "The Leadership Gap," a study performed for the Center for Creative Leadership. This study describes inspiring leaders as those who have a particular knack for motivating others, who paint portraits in which their followers see not only future possibilities for the business, but also promising opportunities for themselves. Inspiring, charismatic leaders communicate in rich tones and harmonies that reach the hearts, minds, and souls of those with whom they share their visions. And by their own example, they create storylines where everyone lives happily ever after.

Sound like a fantasy? It's all completely possible – with just a little inspiration. But inspiration alone doesn't *do* anything. In order to be effective, inspiration must move others to *action*.

The very word "inspire" contains etymological clues for how to make dreams come true and bring art to life. It comes from the Latin word *inspirare*, which means "to breathe upon or into." Breath sustains all life, just as inspiration sparks and sustains creativity. The Latin derivation of breath, *spirare*, is also synonymous with spirit, drawing an analogy between breath, life, and the spirit that moves it. Consequently, one could argue that leadership is as spiritual as it is motivational.

Invoke Your Muse

Journal about your "why." What are your aspirations? What is the guiding reason that motivates the things you want to do? What gives you a sense of urgency?

The leader's challenge is that she has to *both* inspire and be inspired. And where do leaders find this inspiration? They must look inward and answer life's most empowering (and perhaps most perplexing) question – "Why?" Like an artist, the inspired leader has to *see* the picture he wants to paint; he has to *hear* the song he wants to sing and *feel* what his audience or followers feel.

Whether a leader is inspired by his own accessible and available specialists or blessed by the Muse who touches his life in a big way, he needs to ask and answer the question "why?" before he can successfully motivate others to act. Without the *why*, inspiration can become just bells and whistles, to be forgotten the next day. A leader must dig deep and ask,

"*Why* is this cause important? *Why* should we win this game? *Why* should this tool be invented? *Why* should this company accomplish these goals? *Why* do these impossible things need to be done? *Why* should I wake up this morning and do these difficult things? *Why* do I exist?"

In his book *Start With Why*, Simon Sinek explains that leaders who inspire us are not driven by what they do, but by *why* they do it. People *want* to follow leaders who know *why* and who can communicate that vision and passion to their teams. In the early 1980s, Steve Jobs recruited John Sculley, then president of PepsiCo, to become CEO of Apple, a company Jobs started four years prior in his garage. How did Jobs convince this savvy businessman to leave the international beverage giant for a fledgling computer company? He gave Sculley the beginnings of a *why* when he asked him, "Do you want to sell sugar water for the rest of your life, or do you want to come with me and change the world?"

If leaders are not willing and able to breathe inspiration into followers, they will fail, and their organizations will likely *expire*, which literally means to breathe out the last breath. An organization without inspiration is destined for expiration. Though it may remain in business, its spirit will have left for good, resulting in failure to meet mission deadlines, failure to satisfy stakeholders, or inability to meet constituents' needs. And organizations that are unable to breathe in the spirit of rapid change will likely expire sooner than later – like Polaroid, a now-defunct company that failed to anticipate that digital photography would soon bring about its demise.

Over the course of several semesters at Howard University, I studied and translated Virgil's epic poem, *The Aeneid*, in which the lack of a *why* leads to tragedy. The story begins in the middle of the Mediterranean Sea, where the hero, Aeneas, and his fellow Trojans are on a journey to find a place to rebuild their fallen city. On his way to the land that would become Rome, Aeneas meets and falls in love with the young and beautiful Dido, Queen of Carthage. However, when Mercury, the messenger of the gods, reminds Aeneas of his duty, he leaves the love-stricken queen to continue his quest. Broken-hearted, Dido stabs herself with his sword and throws herself upon a burning funeral pyre.

The Aeneid is a story of contrasts – particularly the *pietas* (or mindless duty) of Aeneas, and the *furor* (or frenzied passion) of Dido. In my youth, I understood Dido's *furor*. As she stood on a burning pile of wood and cursed Troy, I could feel the anger delivered by the hard consonants of the Latin and in the deliberate measured rhythm of dactylic hexameter as she curses Aeneas and his descendents – "… *ipsa pyram super ingentem stans saucia Dido mandabat Tyriis ultricia bella futuris…*" But, as a romantic, young woman, I could not understand why Aeneas leaves Dido to resume his journey.

However, in searching for my Leadership Muse, I have found (and am constantly rediscovering) my *why*. Likewise, I now understand Aeneas' *why*. When I asked myself *why* I wanted to write this book, the answer was simple: *Because I HAD to.* And why did Aeneas leave Dido? *Because he HAD to!* Virgil confirms this as he asks rhetorically:

Tell me why, for what attaint of her deity, or in what vexation, did the Queen of heaven drive one so excellent in goodness to circle through so many afflictions, to face so many toils? Is anger so fierce in celestial spirits?

Then he explains:

…ere he might found a city and carry his gods into Latium; from whom is the Latin race, the lords of Alba, and the stately city Rome.

Aeneas' journey was bigger than him, more important than his own desires. On the other hand, Dido forgot her *why*. She forgot her duty to her dead husband's memory, her responsibility to her people, and her vow to sacrifice for the future of her country. One night of passion in a cave caused her to disregard her purpose and destiny.

As leaders, losing sight of *why*, even in the throes of inspiration, spells doom for us and the organizations we lead. Knowing deep down – despite irrational thoughts and sudden, uncontrollable passion – what we must do and the nature of our calling keeps us true.

The *why* for Aeneas, like the *why* for so many of our great and crazy leaders, is akin to a calling. Martin Luther King, Jr., Joan of Arc, and Nelson Mandela – *they did what they did and became who they became because they HAD to.* As you will later read, Queen Bess flew, Vermeer painted, and Grace Hopper programmed – *because they HAD to.* Mother Teresa served, Moses wandered, and the Wright Brothers flew – *because they HAD to.* My grandmother *did* all the many things she did – *because she HAD to.*

In looking for my inspiration, I find it everywhere; it screams from the gentle, whispering inspiration of the Muse. It comes to life in the stories of people who are true to their best selves, their honest *whys*, their greatest aspirations. And as for my own aspirations, I'm not about to let any funeral pyre incinerate my purpose. I breathe in and breathe out the focus and encouragement of my Muse's divine madness, and she helps me turn inspiration into motivation, problems into solutions, plans into actions, vision into reality, and dreams into substance.

chapter 4

INSPIRATION FROM THE MOON AND STARS

"Nothing good can come of this."

DR. ZACHARY SMITH
EVIL VILLAIN IN THE 1998 MOVIE **LOST IN SPACE**

Urania, the ancient Muse of Astronomy, whose name means "heaven," is invoked by those of us with a special interest in the stars. Also associated with universal love and the Holy Spirit, she is usually depicted with a globe in her left hand and her eyes fixed upon the heavens. Her soul, her tones, and her feelings are all reflected in the wisdom we obtain from the sky – wisdom that I wanted even as a youngster.

When I was four years old, I thought I could fly. Just like the young (and careless) Icarus, the ancient archetype of impatient youth who flew too high on homemade wings, I was drawn to the sky but did not realize my own limitations. My tricycle provided wings, and I tested my theory of flight by pushing my spacecraft off the edge of the porch. It sailed in a parabolic path then landed safely on the ground. After several trials, I was ready for my maiden voyage. I got on, peddled fast, sailed off the edge of the porch and dropped straight down. I cried, wounded but not defeated. I knew I could still fly; I just needed a better spacecraft.

The inspiration of Urania called to me, perhaps because fantastic flights of fancy are commonplace in the genre I have always loved – science fiction.

Growing up, I was a fan of *Star Trek, Lost in Space, I Dream of Jeannie*, and other stories of space travel and the creation of a better future. I was slightly younger than Will Robinson's character on TV's *Lost in Space* but I dreamed of a day when I could ride in a space ship and see Earth getting smaller and smaller in the rearview mirror (yes, my imaginary spaceship had a rearview mirror). The thought of an anthropomorphic computer on wheels as a traveling companion appeals to me even to this day. And though the power to blink and solve all my problems was tempting, I never wanted to be Jeannie; I wanted to be Major Nelson – a NASA astronaut. But the force of gravity – and the reality of life – eventually tempered my dream of leaving the atmosphere, and I settled instead for a gig as an entry-level mathematician installing compilers and subroutines, which translate words to computer codes and process data needed to support space flight.

One afternoon many years later, I found myself waiting for a plane from Boston to Washington, D.C., looking up to the sky not with inspired eyes, but with a sense of learned dread. There were thunderstorms in both cities, and one delay would set the traveler's nightmare in motion. Before I even got to the airport, my plane was 15 minutes late. From a seasoned traveler's perspective, this was ominous. When I looked up and saw storm clouds, I hardly suspected there might be something other than bad weather brewing up there. This was a day I feared would become one of the worst days of my life. But my Muse, or perhaps even Urania herself, must have been hovering nearby. This seemingly-bleak day would end up providing a brilliant coda to a story that began nearly three decades before.

When I got to the airport, I was informed that my flight would be an hour late. By the time I checked in, it was two hours behind schedule. No planes were arriving; therefore, no planes were leaving. I was stuck in a secluded terminal with limited amenities and food options, and I was on my perennial low-carbohydrate diet. Still, I had no choice but to wait, and spending the next few hours stewing didn't sound productive, entertaining, or comfortable. Optimism was the better choice – the only choice if I was to salvage the day.

I decided then and there to expect a great day; all I needed to do was search for evidence of its greatness. There were no seats left, so travelers sat on the floor in the corridors, patiently reading, talking, sleeping, and doing all the various things that folks do to pass the time. As I looked around for inspiration, I noticed a lady across from me with a smashed chocolate cupcake in a sealed package. I think it must have said, "Break package only as last resort during emergencies," because she had waited a respectable period of time during our multiple-hour delay. Finally, she broke the package open, ate the smashed cupcake, and declared it the most delicious thing in the universe. Her traveling buddy wasn't too interested. Pleased with his proximity to an electrical outlet, he was distracted, playing a game on his PDA.

Next to me, a seasoned network engineer and retired veteran of our nation's space program told a tall tale from half a century ago. He was fresh out of college and newly employed with NASA when one of his older co-workers took him out for a night on the town in Washington, D.C. in a new sports car convertible with the top down. They had too much to drink and were spotted by a policeman. Rather than pull over, the seasoned journeyman utilized his superior (but compromised) decision-making skills, floored it, and outran the cops. I eventually realized that I actually knew of this daring character. He was a legend and an inspiration to generations of engineers who emulated his daring on the job (but hopefully not on the roads).

As I watched the people around me find little ways to entertain or treat themselves, I was happy to share those inspired moments with them – and to have cashews and water. Optimism appeared to be paying off. It wasn't a bad day filled with flight delays, dehydration, and discomfort; it was a wonderful day of tall tales, smashed cupcakes, and fast convertibles.

Our plane arrived four hours late. In a rare moment of shared joy, we all broke into spontaneous applause. As we boarded, I had the prophetic insight to upgrade to business class, so I looked forward to a very comfortable flight – and a glass of chardonnay. Yes, this was indeed a great day.

I sat next to an old man with a familiar spirit. He reminded me of my grandfather, Daddy Carl. He ordered a Tanqueray and ginger ale, and I got my wine. I made sure that my bag didn't take up his leg room and gave him some advice about his tray table. Then I put on my headset, turned up the volume on my iPod, and looked out the window. Above the storm clouds was a full moon, but its bright light could not dim the sky full of brilliant stars, which reflected off the clouds and gave the illusion of lights against cotton candy.

Invoke Your Muse

Think back to some of the "bad" days you've endured in your leadership career. It could be anything from having terrible sweat stains while delivering a presentation, to a major project failure. Re-imagine these moments as messages from your Muse. What lessons might be hidden in the difficult circumstances?

My mind drifted to the notion that looking up into the sky is actually looking back into the past. The stars we see today are only memories, images of what they looked like when reflected light left them and came into our view at the speed of 186,000 miles per second. Light cannot outrun time, so at this great distance from those heavenly objects, we see what the stars looked like millions of years ago. With Urania at their side, astrologers of old (and many today) divined the future from the light of the past. Little did I know, my Muse was also waiting to reveal a glimpse of *my* past – one that lit the path on my future journey.

We landed and prepared to leave the plane, and I smiled at the familiar, grandfatherly spirit who sat next to me and kept me company. As he pulled his roll-aboard from the overhead compartment, I spied the name on his luggage tag – Kumar. Could it be my old professor? I seized the moment and asked if he taught astronomy at Howard University. He smiled and said that he had but was now retired. He got off the plane before I did, but I found him waiting for me.

As I maneuvered myself off the plane, I remembered another close call for the "worst day of my life," which took place in Dr. Kumar's classroom nearly 30 years earlier. That day, Dr. Kumar asked if we understood the movement of the tides and how the position of the moon, sun, and Earth affected them. Everyone nodded, feigning understanding. Then to my terror, he gave me the chalk and said, "Young lady, explain it to the class."

I said, "OK," and marched to the board, faking confidence. I drew an artful picture of the Earth, moon, and sun, indicating the orbit of the moon around the Earth and the Earth around the sun. While drawing my beautiful orbs, I had time to think about what I was going to say. Finally, having stalled long enough, I explained:

The water on Earth is influenced by the gravitational attraction of the sun and the moon. The moon has the stronger influence because of its proximity to the Earth. The gravitational force pulls the Earth and its waters towards the moon, causing the water to bulge in the direction of the moon's pull. Another bulge occurs on the opposite end of the Earth as the planet moves towards the moon and "away" from the water.

I did not invoke Jeannie, Major Nelson, or Will Robinson, but they were with me that day, bringing my childhood passions to bear on my ability to understand and explain the heavenly bodies. I could tell from Dr. Kumar's smile of approval that he was shocked; my explanation was almost as good as his. Afterwards, my classmates came up to me and said,

"Girl, you did a good job! I'm glad it was you and not me!"

When I caught up with Dr. Kumar all those years later, I shared the story with him. I didn't expect him to remember but I wanted him to know I did. But he did remember. He added, somewhat apologetically (but not really), that the professors were intentionally hard on science and math students at Howard University, because the pressure would make them better in their lives and careers. My old physics professor and his peer, Dr. Anna Coble, regularly gave about 75 students a bad day when she posted grades. He told me she had passed away, but her legacy for tough lessons and sharp students survived.

As for me, I more than survived these "bad" days – strengthened by the trials, challenges, and blessings bestowed on me by a few great professors, Urania, and all the other Muses who have inspired me. As teenagers, we are quick to label an unpleasant situation as "the worst day of my life." But as we age and grow stronger with each "worst day" we overcome, those days start to seem not so bad after all. I came away from that dreadful day in astronomy class loving the moon, stars, sun, tides, and our planet. But I never knew how bright that day was until a dark and stormy night three decades later on the eastern seaboard, a night that promised misery but was punctuated by widely-scattered moments of small inspiration and brief periods of time travel. That night, I realized how much I have been inspired by the magic in the sky. What started out as a bad day for a 17-year-old college freshman would provide a foundation for many good days to come.

The Leadership Muse teaches us that our bad days prepare us for life and toughen us for the leadership trials to come. We grow in our ability to do the difficult things and see challenges in a positive light, so that when it really counts, we can endure and finish the race. As a young coed, I thought that life should be easy. As a prepared and inspired leader, I am grateful for the difficult days that Dr. Kumar and Dr. Coble gave to me;

they were gifts in disguise.

Now, when I look up at the night sky, I think about how it has shaped my history. And I remember being prepared and inspired by a gin-drinking, old sage who sat next to me on a plane 30,000 feet in the air one fateful, stormy night with a full moon.

chapter 5

"I've learned that people will forget what you said,
people will forget what you did, but people
will never forget how you made them feel."

MAYA ANGELOU, AMERICAN POET

People often ask if I have any regrets. One, if not the only one, is that I never took ancient Greek. If I had taken one year of ancient Greek, I would have completed a double major – a Bachelor of Science in Mathematics and a Bachelor of Arts in Classics. With my study of music in high school, I could have considered myself akin to the ancient philosophers – Socrates, Pythagoras, Plato, and Aristotle – who saw integral connections between the stars, music, math, and pure ideas. But alas, as a 20-year-old college student, I thought more of trivial things like sleep, or about how maybe I could see exploding chests and Sigourney Weaver in *Alien* one more time on a big screen and with larger-than-life sound at the Uptown Theater in northwest Washington, D.C. And because my 1970 Dodge Dart 225 Slant Six needed a new radiator and master cylinder, I also thought about looking for a job. All of these things seemed more important than two semesters studying another dead language.

Had I mastered the Greek language, I could truly be like Pythagoras, a major thinker in his day (roughly 570 to 480 B.C.) and an inspiration for lovers of knowledge and wisdom for centuries to come. A mathematician and philosopher who discovered and named many important principles of mathematics and acoustics, Pythagoras believed in practicing silence and studying math, and in the therapeutic importance of music. He was also powerfully charismatic. Some even considered him mystical, and in many ways, he was treated as a holy man.

Charisma, a term made relevant by turn-of-the-century German sociologist Max Weber, is a personality trait in individuals who are set apart from others by their ability to inspire or incite people to action. People are drawn or attracted to charismatic individuals, those who have leadership authority and are often thought to be touched by divine madness or blessed with mystical powers.

However, many think of charisma as a negative quality of leadership, because it is often associated with the blind devotion of mindless followers. David Koresh and Jim Jones, who each inspired the mass suicide of his followers, are examples of charisma gone awry. Jim Collins, author of *Good to Great*, warns against "the dangers of entrusting our future to self-serving leaders who use our institutions ... whether in the corporate or social sectors ... to advance their own interests."

However, when used for good, charisma can help inspire people to do their best, to feel good about themselves, and to understand where and why you are leading them. John C. Maxwell, author of *The 21 Indispensible Qualities of a Leader*, lists charisma as one of the most important leadership qualities and insists that it is a trait one can develop and improve upon, not just something you must be born with.

Essentially, your charisma (or your "gift of grace," as derived from the Greek root) has everything to do with how you learn to love life, which is exactly what Maxwell encourages leaders to do. People are attracted to people who are happy and cheerful, who treat them kindly and make them feel good about themselves. This means being optimistic and seeing the goodness and inspiration in everything and everyone around us. Players on a football team want to feel like they will win; employees in a large corporation want to believe that the company will make a profit and be successful; and people suffering through the tyranny of oppression need to have faith that better days will come. In order to inspire motivation, change, innovation, invention, or anything else worth inspiring, one must first be able to see it as a possibility. A charismatic leader has vision, joy, hope, and optimism, and these characteristics inspire others to follow.

In order to achieve this general sense of well being, Maxwell encourages leaders to "put a 10 on everyone's head" and see everyone as the best they could possibly be. And who doesn't want to be with, or even serve, people who see us in such a positive light? We all crave the priceless gift of hope – to be inspired with an expectation of a brighter tomorrow. Charismatic leaders know this, and they paint positive pictures of us and our futures; they can make us feel and *believe* in possibilities and in our own potential as individuals and as groups.

Author and spiritualist Marianne Williamson relates charisma to "letting God's light shine through us." Charisma is like sunlight, which shines on and warms us. And just as the sun has a gravitational pull that attracts other heavenly bodies, the charisma of the leader acts like a divine, invisible energy, drawing in and inspiring his followers.

Without a focus on empowering others, the power of charisma can turn dangerous. Charisma, when it goes awry, turns into a black hole of bad leadership, sucking in people who are mindlessly devoted to someone who does not care about their well-being. True charisma requires the ability to inspire through the grace of *being* inspired. The charismatic leader doesn't have to be perfect, but she must be unselfish and willing to share herself – like Pythagoras, who didn't hoard his inspiration to leverage power and influence over others. Instead, he shared his wisdom *and* his time with the men and women he inspired, and his influence has endured for thousands of years.

chapter 6

*"Never underestimate the power of dreams and the
influence of the human spirit. We are all the same in this notion:
The potential for greatness lives within each of us."*

WILMA RUDOLPH, 1960 OLYMPIC CHAMPION IN TRACK AND FIELD
("THE FASTEST WOMAN IN THE WORLD")

More than 2,500 years after Pythagoras' time, I was admiring the freshness of the produce in Costco when I spied a man who seemed familiar.
A polished man in his late forties, he had an engaging smile, and his long
forehead gave him a distinguished look. As I approached him, we exchanged a look of mutual recognition. He didn't remember my name,
but he said, "The only person on earth who speaks Latin!"

"Mene memoria tenetis?" I said, which literally translated from Latin to
English means "Do you hold me in your memory?" I could see him men-
tally roll his eyes, wondering what I said. "Do you remember me?" I asked,
and we both laughed.

I remembered him as a seventh-grade boy in Mr. Cave's Latin class at
Kelly Miller Junior High School in Washington, D.C. When we studied
the Olympics, Mr. Cave planned a special game day for the class. We had

to participate in the long jump, toss the shot put, and throw the discus. And we could only speak Latin that day. It was one of the best days of my life, because I was the only one in class talking. For some reason, my former classmate didn't hold this memory as fondly as I did.

That day, my 12-year-old imagination carried me back into past centuries to bask in the victory of my Olympic performance. I imagined myself not just an Olympic champion, but also a Greek or Roman goddess. Yes, I was Athena – virgin, Greek goddess, athletic, smart, crafty, and an inspiration to heroes – or Minerva, her Roman counterpart. All I needed was a helmet, a quiver of arrows, and an owl – or a bedroom sheet that functioned smartly as a toga.

Nearly 40 years later, on a Mediterranean cruise that would take me and my mother to the site of the first Olympic games, I harbored the hope that I would finally, through some stroke of inspiration, get back in touch with the neglected Greek goddess in me. I was excited to stand on that ancient playing field with the spirit of the ancient Greeks and feel the inspiration of Pythagoras and Socrates, who may have walked the same dusty roads I would travel to get there.

Invoke Your Muse

How is your leadership journey comparable to an Olympic event? Is it a marathon? A discus toss? A long poetry recitation? How have you honed your natural abilities and trained yourself for leadership?

As we entered the park, my mother said it reminded her of a cemetery. She was deceived by the remains of the marble columns, now marble blocks strewn across the grounds. To her, the park seemed dead; to me,

LC IN KATAKOLON (OLYMPIA), GREECE 2010.

in this place where long-forgotten athletes from across the known world came together in a spirit of peace and camaraderie, the air was thick with echoes of inspiration.

The ancient Olympics began around 800 B.C. as a series of athletic competitions between Greek states. If any of the states were at war with one another, an Olympic truce was called, and peace prevailed during the competition. Athletic events included racing, wrestling, long jump, javelin throwing, and discus tossing. Winners received and proudly wore olive wreaths. In addition, artists and poets would bring their works to share at the international gathering.

As I walked through the groves of olive and pecan trees and heard the snap and crackle of fallen pecans under my feet, I could *smell* the relics from thousands of years of victory. The breeze carried the sweet voice of the Hero's Muse, rousing men's souls to persevere over defeat, to follow the rules of the games, and to believe in themselves and their abilities. I felt the lingering spirit of hope that still occupied the clearings and walkways, a reminder of the time when athletes laid down their arms to perform their personal best. Athletes prepared, trained, and pushed through physical pain because they were inspired by hope, an intense desire to triumph, and the expectation of victory.

I couldn't help but pause at the entrance of the Olympic stadium and express with my arms stretched up to heavens the joy that every successful leader feels – victory. And it turns out that I knew just enough ancient Greek to read a few inscriptions and understand the ancient wisdom at the Heraion, the ancient temple of Hera, queen of the gods. This was where the Olympic heroes celebrated their victories. Whether a Hera in 600 B.C. or a Hero in 2011 A.D., we all need to pause long enough to acknowledge the successful end to each challenging journey.

As our cruise ship set sail that night, I watched the sun set and the moon rise over the Aegean Sea. As the stars began to peek out, I imagined hearing the Pythagorean diatonic music of the spheres. And that night, I had a dream about the goddess Athena. She stood over me and watched me as I slept. Her helmet hid her face but couldn't hide the beauty and wisdom that came from her spirit. I don't remember anything else about the dream but I woke up feeling refreshed and inspired. I guess I didn't need ancient Greek after all; I had my Olympic victory. I was more than an athlete; I was the goddess of inspiration for athletes and heroes for years to come.

chapter 7

"And the highest point of my art is the power to prove by every test
whether another's thought is a false phantom or instinct with life and
truth. The admirable truths they bring to birth have been discovered by
themselves from within. But the delivery is heaven's work and mine."

SPOKEN BY SOCRATES IN PLATO'S **THEAETETUS**

A recent technology conference in Dallas, Texas, (for which I had to put my Redskins team spirit in suspended animation) focused on how leaders could incorporate new and emerging technologies into their organizations. Buzz about "ideation," or the process of creating ideas, was all over the place. Folks were talking about how to use the generation of ideas to feed the technology-adoption life cycle, which starts with the birth of an idea and is then evaluated by a set of guinea pigs. If an idea survives these initial stages, it must achieve sustained use by early adopters. Then, in its final test of viability, it must be accepted by the mainstream.

This recurring conversation kept reminding me of a book I'd recently read, *History of the Telephone*, written in 1910 by Herbert N. Casson. I couldn't help but notice the parallels between social media and the adoption of the great, "new" invention of the late 1800s – the phone. All the hype around social media (blogging, "tweeting" in 140 characters or less to communicate fast and personally, and using Facebook or LinkedIn to reach out in powerful ways) sounded a lot like the pre-World War I excitement Casson writes about.

I had *déjà vu*. But I was alone in this feeling that we'd all been here before. All around me, people were talking about innovation as if it was something *new*. People were throwing around the concept of ideation as if it was a cutting-edge discovery, not just a fancy word describing the creation of ideas, something man has been doing throughout history. Though the conference was fascinating, I found the hype of ideation rather tiresome. According to Myers-Briggs, my personality profile is INTP (introverted, intuitive, thinking, and perceptive). I am supposed to be perceptive and curious – an idea-generating machine. So why was I uncomfortable in the midst of all this hoopla? Why did I feel like I was the only one not drinking the Kool-Aid?

The notion of ideation had been bugging me for a while, but I really couldn't put my finger on why until I read *Closing the Innovation Gap*. In it, author Judy Estrin quotes Andy Grove, retired CEO of Intel:

There are a half a dozen words in the English language that are substitutes for substance. Three of them are innovation, accountability, and leadership. Companies that let people get away with murder talk too much about accountability. Those that don't have the courage to leave the handrail talk incessantly about leadership. And people who are incapable of changing what they are doing, or even analyzing what's wrong, go on and on about innovation.

The words themselves are the trouble, I realized, especially when buzz words take the place of the real deal and talking takes the place of doing. What good are ideas if they lack substance and never develop into anything of measured value or provide learning opportunities? And then again, what if you're on the brink of a life-altering idea but grow weary and stop just short of that "eureka" moment, aborting a great idea? In these moments, the Leadership Muse departs, her attempts to inspire having been spurned by the very people who needed her help.

When *Time* magazine recognized the "50 Best Inventions of 2008," the article discussed what Estrin calls an *ecosystem*, a creative environment which breeds the marvelous engineering wonders of the world. In biology, an ecosystem is a complex community of organisms and their shared environment. In organizations, Estrin defines it as it relates to "collaborative organisms," which include "scientists, product developers, businesspeople, service providers, and customers, all of whom participate in one or more of three communities: research, development, and application."

Invoke Your Muse

Think about ideas that you have witnessed being born. Which ones survived, and which did not? Did some not make it that should have? Was there a leadership process in place to determine the viability of ideas so that strong ones didn't get neglected?

Two missions from NASA made *Time*'s list: the Lunar Reconnaissance Orbiter (#3), which explored the lunar surface for possible landing sites and probable locations of water, and the Mars Science Laboratory (#18), which carried a suite of instruments to give us more insight into the Martian environment. Also on the list was Google's Floating Data Center (#47), which patented floating islands of servers on barges, using the resources of the ocean for power and cooling.

Creatively-inspired ecosystems like these generate innovation and ideas that can change the world, but only if their leaders know how to create and nurture them. Consistent, great innovation comes about as a result of a leader creating the right environment, for the right people, given the right resources. The people of NASA and Google had the courage to persist, fueled by passion and inspired by nurturing leaders who struck the right balance of questioning, risk-taking, deliberateness, and trust. It takes this nurturing to sustain inspiration from the drawing board to the finish line, where we learn from failures as well as from successes, or, in moments of divine genius, where we see ideas take flight. And for a leader to claim that he is responsible for his team's innovation, without dutiful and inspired action, is like the rooster taking credit for the sunrise. In those cases, innovation just happens, and the lazy leader crows about it – and often falls short of doing what needs to be done to make the ideas a reality.

Ideation is just a word. Or worse, uninspired ideation is a mindless but dutiful paint-by-numbers process where, like an artist without the blessing of the Muse, you cover all the numbers with the right colors to create a recognizable picture, but one that will never become a great work. On the other hand, it's also doubtful that throwing paint up against a canvass in a frenzied way could accidently produce what some call art. However, when the invisible hand and influence of the Leadership Muse are at work, we, the leaders, see masterpieces develop on the canvases of the organizations we lead. And those of us who have the courage to follow the divine inner voice of inspiration will see our teams begin to bring our visions to life.

In one of Plato's dialogues, the *Theaetetus*, Socrates compares the art of philosophy to the art of midwifery. A midwife helps women give birth safely, bringing into the world that which has already come to life within a pregnant mother. Similarly, Socrates defines the role of a philosopher (his own profession) as one who helps others *give birth* to the ideas they have within them. While some ideas are stillborn, or "phantoms," others are alive and real. And philosophers help people discern which ideas are substantial enough to have lives of their own.

Like the midwife and the philosopher, the artful and inspirational leader will help her followers bring forth the truth, passion, and knowledge that is within them so that they may give birth to new ideas, ideas that will grow up to become desired outcomes. The leader who invokes her Muse will understand how to apply the right dose of motivation, power, and purpose to inspire ideas capable of growing into masterpieces of innovation. Now, *that's* something to crow about.

chapter 8

STUPID IDEAS

*"We found, instead, that they first got the right people on the bus,
the wrong people off the bus, and the right people in the right seats.
And then they figured out where to drive it."*

JIM COLLINS
AUTHOR OF **GOOD TO GREAT**

For thousands of years, artistic and scientific creativity has been associated with the influence of the Muse. The madness that occurs when the Muse's inspiration takes hold requires discernment as much as it necessitates freedom. That's why it's important to recognize the misguided, half-baked outcomes and distinguish them from the labor pains that give birth to the divine emanations of the Muse. And as we struggle to listen to the tiny whispers of our Muses, we need to reduce the "noise" – the uninspired and artificial processes that hamper the journey to divine perfection and the distractions that can be caused by the wrong people, the wrong motives, or even our own egos.

Assuming we are able to get beyond the mindless duty of *ideation*, isn't it still possible to end up with something utterly ridiculous? A whole school of thought proclaims that there are no stupid ideas. I beg to differ. Stupid ideas come from stupid people. But before I describe the unmistakable characteristics of stupid people, let's talk about stupid ideas.

I happened upon a Stupid Idea Generator (Dix) on the Internet that was no doubt constructed by innovative people only pretending to be stupid. Some of my favorites were: glass hammer, concrete parachute, three-way mirror, six-foot bonsai tree, and (my favorite) etch-a-sketch checkbook. The website also listed the disposable computer as a silly idea, but as an IT leader in the public sector, I think this one has merit! Consider the laptop. No matter what brand or version you buy, or how much money you spend, or how well you take care of it, the technology will become obsolete – but not before you screech to a halt, run out of disc space, and exceed the relative capacity of the technology. Whether the laptop is expensive or cheap, the same outcome awaits: You will need to buy another laptop. So if you, like most people, use your computer to run simple software and surf the Web, why not spend less for a capable and reliable disposable computer, as opposed to an expensive one that is more "long term" (i.e., a few years)?

Sometimes ideas that sound stupid turn out to be the kind of out-of-the-box thinking that produces amazing results. Notwithstanding the disposable computer, there have been several ideas that *seemed* stupid but ended up making millions of dollars. Sometimes your Muse will whisper an idea that would sound like nonsense to anyone but you. Through her grace and your dedication, you will take her inspiration and create a remarkable outcome. Consider, for example, doggie goggles, antenna balls, and personalized letters to Santa – all of which are now money-making inventions. No doubt the first people to suggest selling bottled water got a few strange looks and heard "Who would pay for water?" more than once. But the thinkers behind all of these "stupid ideas" listened only to the voices of their Muses. And who's laughing now?

Even if your off-beat idea doesn't hit the jackpot, don't despair. Sometimes ideas that seem to be failures end up becoming learning opportunities on the path to greatness. Thomas Edison gave birth to many "stillborn" ideas as he learned, through trial and error, what was needed to invent the light bulb, the phonograph, and the motion-picture camera. No one would dare call Thomas Edison stupid.

What, then, defines stupidity? Not failures and not I.Q. Stupid people are not those who lack education or intellect. Very intelligent people can be stupid. Similarly, people with low intellect or poor education can produce brilliant ideas that work. But most stupid people have a few things in common:

"STUPID" PEOPLE DON'T SEEK DIVERSITY. They will often ask other stupid people if their ideas are good. In other words, they only seek advice from people in their own inner circles, which tend to be made up of people who think, act, and maybe even look like them. Stupid people only want opinions that confirm their social construct of reality.

Invoke Your Muse

Do you know any "stupid" people – people who shy away from diversity of thought, approaches, or ideas? Think of major project or initiative failures that could have been prevented with a different team composition. How can you operate in a manner that gets the right people on the team?

Smart people and leaders know that diversity matters when it comes to innovation – in terms of demographics (i.e., gender, race, and age), life experiences, thought patterns, belief systems, and perspectives. For example, a study by the National Center for Women & Information Technology shows that diverse teams including women are more successful at producing patentable ideas with practical outcomes. While it is very comforting to be in the land of the familiar with the usual suspects, surrounding yourself with and getting feedback from people who are different from you can help you make a good idea great – and that's smart. It has been shown over and again that culturally diverse, multidisciplinary teams out-perform homogenous ones.

"STUPID" PEOPLE DON'T LISTEN. Whether out of delusion, cognitive dissonance, or righteous arrogance, stupid people defend their ideas without listening to advice or feedback. They care more about sounding brilliant and being able to say it was all their idea than actually producing results. These folks are like the thinkers who Socrates' says give birth to phantoms – all bluster and no substance.

My husband and I joke that one shouldn't give drunk or crazy people a microphone. They want to hear themselves speak, but they rarely have anything worthwhile to say. A myth of the 1960s culture was that drugs or alcohol make you more creative. But research indicates that it doesn't; it just makes people think your behavior is altered or that you are, in fact, high. People who would rather defend ideas that don't work rather than listen to feedback that could produce desired results are like drunks with microphones or pothead poets; they think they are brilliant but they are all bluster and really just annoying. As the noble Englishman, Disraeli, once said of his contemporary, the19th century politician, Gladstone: "He is a sophistical rhetorician inebriated by his own verbosity."

"STUPID" PEOPLE DON'T LEARN FROM MISTAKES. Those who do not learn from the past are condemned to repeat it," said the philosopher Santayana, providing us with a succinct definition of stupidity. Very successful people often fall into this trap because they become arrogant or self-righteous about past triumphs. Because they have had so much experience creating good results, they never get into the disciplined habit of learning from their mistakes. Like the "one-hit wonder" bands who make it big with a great song or album and then disappear from the charts forever, thinkers who start off their careers with a bang often stall before reaching the next level of excellence. History's consistently great thinkers – Edison, Einstein, Walt Disney, Henry Ford, Gandhi – all struggled and failed, learning something each time … and then they changed the world.

"STUPID" PEOPLE GET ON THE WRONG BUS. In *Good to Great*, Jim Collins talks about some of the critical actions to make a good company great, including "getting the right people on the bus." To derive the best outcomes from innovation, leaders must first make sure there are no stupid people on their buses. Stupid leaders surround themselves with people who think like them – who don't care about the outcome and don't learn from mistakes. The potentially-great leader will assemble a high-functioning team by interviewing people and checking their references so that she can identify those with diverse backgrounds and the right academic/work credentials. She will also listen to her instincts, or the tiny voice of the Leadership Muse. The Muse may reveal that someone with lukewarm references and a degree from a low-quality institution, or who seems too young or too old, is the right person for the team. Likewise, the Muse may reveal that the seemingly crack-pot idea an interviewee shares is actually a stroke of genius. When that happens, don't be stupid. Listen.

chapter 9

APPROACHING INFINITY WITH YOUR MUSE

"To dream anything that you want to dream.
That's the beauty of the human mind.
To do anything that you want to do.
That is the strength of the human will.
To trust yourself and test your limits.
That is the courage to succeed."

BERNARD EDMONDS, AUTHOR AND MUSICIAN

As a college hopeful, I spent my teenage years feeling like I was poised on the threshold of big dreams where the sky was the limit. Though I knew college was something my family probably couldn't afford, I never doubted that I would be able to surpass the obstacles blocking my goals. And my big dream of going to college came true – early, in fact. I was selected to be one of four high-school seniors admitted into the D.C. public school system's High-School College Internship Program. The four of us spent our 12th-grade year as freshmen at Howard University, carrying full class loads on full scholarships. And at 17 years old, I entered my very first calculus course.

Calculus talks about complex and grand ideas such as limits and infinity. Just a year earlier, as a high-school junior, I didn't know my limits or understand how big infinity really could be. So when I was accepted into this program, I was excited to explore the subject matter of mathematicians like Newton and Pythagoras. My calculus professor was a handsome, young man from Jamaica. Though his accent was rather British, at least to my American ear, his unrestrained and infectious passion for mathematics was often articulated in a snappy Caribbean staccato. During one noteworthy class, this particular professor discussed the concept of *infinity*. He asked me in the lyrical rhythm of the Jamaican patois, "You tink anyting biggah den infinity, Miss?"

I didn't get it. Was it a number? Was it a really, really big number? How big was it? This concept of the infinite was so foreign and elusive – yet critical in understanding calculus. How can you get infinitely close to something, never to reach it? What does it mean to be infinitely small or infinitely large? All these questions I pondered, and all these answers I sought. If I was to surpass my limits, I needed to understand infinity.

So I asked him, "How big is infinity?"

In his sassy, West-Indian brogue, he said, "It's as big as you like, Miss."

"How big is that?" I insisted.

"*Very* big," he replied.

I stared at him, perplexed and frustrated. He asked me to think of the greatest number I could imagine. I did. Then he told me infinity was greater than that! It seemed to me that numbers should have an upper limit. Man could not really fathom measurement to be so vast, and if he could not fathom it, how could it even be useful?

He told me to think about my "greatest number" and then add a little bit more to it, (for example, $n + 1$, where n is the greatest number you can imagine). It gets even bigger when you add something to it, so it can't possibly be the biggest. And if you keep adding to it, you get to a place symbolized by ∞.

I left class unsatisfied with his answers. Still perplexed, I visited him during his office hours (several times, in fact). Our conversations about infinity drifted to notions of the vastness of the universe, the unbounded nature of unconditional love, and the enormous power of God. I began to realize that unlike calculus, the human mind puts limits on itself. We put initial conditions on our lives, imagining barriers: we can't do this thing, or women can't do that thing, or we'll never be able to accomplish that outcome. Yet, in the calculus of our lives, greatness is achieved when we aim for infinity – and beyond. Infinity is big enough to hold all you can imagine and more, so vast that it surpasses any effort to grasp it – or reach it. As we look to infinity, the possibilities become endless, and our abilities become unbounded.

When we apply calculus to leadership and personal performance, our abilities and possibilities become as big as infinity. Instead of assuming there are upper bounds on our capabilities, we can just add a little something (n + inspiration + perspiration + passion) and achieve more than we even imagined. Leaders who understand and harness this magic can accomplish the impossible. They capture the hearts, minds, and souls of the people they lead (because even people who don't believe in magic *want* to). And they know that little bit to add, over and over again, to approach infinity.

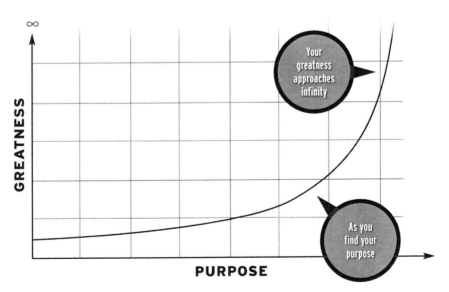

APPROACHING GREATNESS ASYMPTOTICALLY AS YOU SEE YOUR PURPOSE.

chapter 10

"Fortisimmo at last!"

GUSTAV MAHLER, AUSTRIAN COMPOSER AND CONDUCTOR

In April 1977, I witnessed an inspired teacher, deeply in touch with his Leadership Muse, as he harnessed the infinite potential of a group of teenage musicians. Duke Ellington School of Arts High School in Washington, D.C., was only three years old the year that our concert band participated in an annual competition at the Apple Blossom Festival in Winchester, Virginia.

Unlike the other schools in the competition, we couldn't afford uniforms. Nevertheless, our director, Mr. Clark, wanted us to look sharp. The boys wore rented tuxedos, and the girls wore long, black skirts – many of which we (or our mothers) made. We were underdogs – an urban, fledgling school with homemade skirts, borrowed instruments, and a lot of heart.

Mr. Clark instilled in all of us the need to win. He explained that because we were a young school, and under constant threat of being abolished due to the public school system's budget challenges, it was important that we make a good showing to prove that this experimental educational concept – to create a public school of fine arts in Washington, D.C. – would bear fruit. The school selected top students through a competitive audition, created a relaxed, safe atmosphere in which to learn the finer points of the fine arts, and nurtured budding artists on a steady diet of quality education and artistic training. My senior class was the first grad-uating class, and we had to lead the way for others.

My best girlfriend, Donna, and I comprised the highly-accomplished French horn section – in its entirety. However, in our senior year, we were both participating in the full-time college internship program. Our part-time enrollment in the high school made Mr. Clark nervous, so he re-cruited two beginners to round out our section. They were awful. They had poor pitch and could barely read music, which would surely jeopardize our ability to win. We *had* to win this competition, so Donna and I pulled the newbies aside and threatened them with death if they played during our competition. We told them to simply hold their horns erect and pretend they were playing. They wisely obeyed ... at least during rehearsals.

Invoke Your Muse
Think about a Cinderella story, whether it's yours or someone else's. Absent a fairy godmother, what leadership actions made it possible for everyone to live happily ever after?

I drove my mother's 1972 Ford Torino Squire, packed with eight of my closest friends, to and from rehearsals, an additional five hours of practice after school each day. My brother, David, with his euphonium, and my sis-ter, Loreen, with her clarinet, also squeezed into our happy carpool. Ex-hausted but light of heart and satisfied after rehearsals, we'd walk the dark cobblestone streets of Georgetown, eerie and heavy with the humidity of the Potomac River. After dropping everyone off safely, Loreen, David and I would arrive home as late as 10:00 p.m. to complete homework and hit the sewing machine. Yeah, we were underdogs, and we didn't have a strong chance of winning, but we would look really cute in those black skirts – as long as I could sew a straight seam.

As we prepared for our performance that warm day in late April, we hardly noticed that we were the most racially-diverse band, the only ones in homemade concert attire, and the smallest group, relative to the other obviously well-financed bands. But to our credit, we had the only contrabass clarinet in the competition and were the coolest, by far.

When it was our turn to perform, Mr. Clark stepped on the podium, and our collective adrenalin surged. He raised his baton and took a deep breath. I noticed the baton shaking in his hand to the rapid beat of his nerves, much faster than thirty-second notes. He took another breath and looked at us. He was so … human. Inspired and in love with the music, Mr. Clark heard the divine voice that stirred the passion in his soul; his Leadership Muse was on the scene. He wanted us to win for ourselves. We wanted to win for *him*, and the passion on his face that day fueled our desire. He exhaled and dropped the baton, signaling the downbeat and the beginning of our concert.

We played "The Footlifter March" by Henry Fillmore at a perfectly-crisp and characteristically-fast tempo. But suddenly, there was a beautiful sound I had not heard before. Where did the rich brass section come from? And what of those beautiful French horns? Our next song was "People" by Styne and Merrill, and we were the luckiest *people* in the world that day. The normally goofy and attention-challenged cymbal player hit his cue at exactly the perfect moment to send chills and goose bumps up the spines of our audience members.

And there it was … again and again – that strange, rich, beautiful sound coming from the French horn section. Suddenly, I realized that the unfamiliar, sweet sound was coming from four people playing French horns, instead of just the two *prima donas*. We discovered later that the newbies had gotten together and put in many extra hours of practice so they could perform their personal best. It was magical and divine.

After the last band played, we listened eagerly as the judges announced the scores. The bands were rated on a scale of one to three, one being the coveted high mark. The big band with the nice uniforms got a "two"; so did the other band. We held our breath as they announced our score. We got a "one"?! Could it be? We did the impossible? We won!

Later, we listened to a recording of our performance dubbed over with the judge's comments. They noted the "mellifluous tones" of the French horn section. The two beginners were awful musicians; yet together, we sounded *so* beautiful. The euphonium section, led by my brother, sang well-executed riffs in "The Footlifter March." The tempo of the percussion section was crisp and exact, and our new contrabass clarinet player found his voice through his moist reed and the rich, deep tones of his instrument.

Needless to say, Duke Ellington School of the Arts not only survived; it began to thrive. In later years, its show choir and the jazz ensemble also gained notoriety, and people began to expect a high level of performance from its students. I credit that divine spring day in 1977, when a small group of humble band students and a devoted, inspired conductor did what was unexpected in Shenandoah Valley – surpassed imposed limits and began what has continued to be a legacy in education for the performing arts.

That band concert taught me three of the most important lessons I have ever learned about leadership, approaching infinity, and bringing an impossible dream into reality.

DOING THE IMPOSSIBLE REQUIRES BEING PREPARED, both through conscientious training and summoning the courage and willingness to *act* at the required time. The awful French horn players knew they were bad, but they prepared and were powerfully motivated to be part of a winning team. That day, they refused to be mere horn-holders. Instead, they were heroes.

CHAPTER 10

DOING THE IMPOSSIBLE REQUIRES FOCUSED PASSION and the collective will to act with confidence and competence. The goofy cymbal player, who usually paid attention to everything around him *except* his music, was so inspired by our collective, mounting anticipation and desire to win that he was able to focus like a laser for 30 minutes. He took his cue from the entire band, and our perfectly-executed crescendo climaxed with the flawlessness of his precise and graceful cymbal crash. Despite his inability to pay attention, he couldn't ignore the band's unified and focused passion.

DOING THE IMPOSSIBLE REQUIRES A LEADERSHIP MUSE. Mr. Clark's selfless, inspirational leadership kept us focused on what we *all* wanted – to win. As a group, we had enough musical experience to know what it was like to suffer through the temperamental mood swings of some narcissistic directors. But Mr. Clark was motivated to inspire, help, and lead *us* – each of us. He chose diverse music that complemented our musical strengths; he was innovative enough to turn a mediocre clarinet player into a star on the contrabass clarinet. Touched both by Euterpe, the Muse of Music, and his personal Leadership Muse, Mr. Clark took our limited skill, size, and funds and orchestrated them into the infinite harmony that made our impossible victory a certainty.

chapter 11

NOTHING IS RANDOM

"Anyone who considers arithmetical methods of producing random digits is, of course, in a state of sin."
JOHN VON NEUMANN, MATHEMATICIAN AND COMPUTER SCIENTIST

Believing in the power of the Leadership Muse means believing in the infinite and the impossible, and this requires not believing in randomness. "Random" suggests that luck is an important element in accomplishing the impossible or improbable. If we believe that the impossible can happen at random, then as leaders, we won't be motivated to *act*, to meet challenges and work to achieve desired results. We could just cross our fingers and hope for a desired outcome. Maybe we would get lucky, and it might "randomly" happen, but then it would not be our victory to claim. Even worse than crossing fingers, we might become paralyzed into inaction, waiting for funds, resources, another job, a ship to come in. . . and another and another. Napoleon Hill, in *Think and Grow Rich*, observes that people who believe that success requires luck are almost always disappointed. They don't realize that good luck grows from seeds of discernment, determination, passion, and obsession.

While I loved almost all subjects in mathematics, I always hated statistics. I understood it – the concepts, rules, application, and theories. Yet, I never liked it – that science of defining the probability that something will or will not happen by chance. I always had my doubts that anything could be truly random, because God, as Albert Einstein says, "does not play dice." Not only had I never encountered a Muse of Statistics, but I seriously doubted one could even exist. The work of the Muses seems to fly in the face of randomness and chance. The Leadership Muse, for example, *defies* probability and does her best work when no one expects it, except, of course, the leader who listens faithfully for her voice.

Early in my career as a systems programmer for the Department of Justice, one of my customers reported that the random-number generator on our system was defective. Every time he invoked the function, he could predict the result. And if he could predict the result, he explained, it could not be random.

I reviewed the computer's programming language source code in order to explain it to him. The generator was programmed to grab some machine storage, load it in a register, flip some bits, and shift things around a few times – and then, like magic, a "random" number would appear. The problem was not with the machine but with the accuracy of its name. In truth, the number wasn't really random when you understood how it was created. If you loaded a predetermined piece of data (a "seed") into the machine, you would get the same "random" number on every subsequent try.

I called my customer and provided this unsatisfying explanation, and our conversation quickly devolved into a pointless philosophical conversation on the meaning of "random." In that moment, I finally figured out why I hate statistics; I don't believe in randomness. So I ended the telephone call asserting that we had hit upon the reason that there was really no such thing as randomness.

At the time, I was working on my master's degree in Applied Mathematics. After class that night, I impulsively decided to stay and chat with the professor, to whom I declared that I hated statistics because it requires a fundamental assumption of randomness. I told him about my unsatisfied customer and said I didn't believe anything could be random, though I couldn't say why. He said, "Oh, that's easy. You believe in God."

That made sense. I suppose that if one really believes that God "seeds" events, or at least has faith (as I do) that something much bigger than us can overcome the roll of the dice, nothing *would* seem random.

Invoke Your Muse

Do you experience entropy, chaos, or randomness in your work? Re-imagine the randomness. Trusting in your Muse and leadership skills, what are some concrete actions you could take to reclaim order and change your destiny?

In ancient mythology and science, we often find concepts of randomness and fate intertwined to the point that randomness is explained away through both natural and supernatural processes. If things are not random, not a result of chance, they are predetermined. Chance, in the ancient tales and in science, is often not chance at all, but an intense series of foreboding circumstances. The mythological Furies bring bad luck to the heroine who betrays her father for her lover. A whole countryside seems cursed with a mysterious disease that actually comes from an overpopulation of rats with fleas. When they see devotion, the Muses swoop in with inspiration, even though it seems to come from out of nowhere. Fate or destiny tie *seemingly* random events, and sometimes avoidable acts, together to create a divine logic and justify the existence of divine will.

People once accepted and even rejoiced in this. But today, we struggle with the notion of randomness versus fate, because both possibilities seem to take control away from us and undermine the roles we play in determining our own futures. We think that if things happen at random, then nothing we do matters. On the other hand, if something is predetermined, either by divine or human intervention, it seems futile to try and create any other outcome.

I understand the if/then reasoning at work here, but it's more complicated than that. The second law of thermodynamics tells us about *entropy* – promising us that things will go from a state of order to a state of disorder unless we perform some action, often one requiring will power and personal determination. Action does not produce random results, nor is it void against a predetermined outcome. But many of today's leaders have lost touch with their Muses and slipped into a lazy way of being wherein everything appears random, simply because they are not taking inspired action for which they can see measurable results. Inspired leaders must listen to their Muses and work to shape their own destinies.

If we do not believe in or understand divine concepts such as the power of faith and its infinite potential, if we do not invoke a Muse every now and then and seek unexpected inspiration, or if we do not appreciate the infinite potential of the individual and individuals who come together as teams, we are condemned to the hopeless chaos of blind destiny. Perhaps infinity is where the spiritual self and the potential self both dwell.

The leader who listens to her Muse will think big – then bigger than that, then bigger than even that. She will believe that she can make a difference. She will not leave results to random chance – which includes crossing fingers, flipping a coin, rolling the dice, or even buying a lottery ticket. She will know her own powers and gifts and *act* to attain her desired outcome – to embody the greatest leadership possible.

part two
Lessons from the Muse

chapter 12

RIGHT-BRAINED MUSES FOR LEFT-BRAINED HEROES

*"Logical and precise, left-brain thinking gave us the Information Age.
Now comes the Conceptual Age — ruled by artistry, empathy, and emotion."*

DAN PINK, AUTHOR OF **A WHOLE NEW MIND**

When I was a little girl, my mother and grandmother took me with
them on shopping trips to the O Street Market in northwest Washington,
D.C. What I loved most about these outings was not the opportunity to
push through the crowded marketplace and enjoy the distinct aroma of
fish and others meats at various stages of freshness. No, I found my joy at
the edge of the parking lot, playing in the Kennedy Playground. I flew on
planes and rode trains. I imagined soaring high over Washington, D.C.,
and looking down on all the people and cars. On the train, I could prac-
tically feel the gentle rocking to and fro and hear the distinct, calming
sound of "choo-choo."

When I was 16 years old, with the newly-acquired ability to drive myself around, I went back to O Street. I was shocked and disappointed to
discover that the trains did not move and planes did not fly. For a moment, I thought maybe they had been replaced with make-believe repli-
cas by a cruel killjoy after some careless children hurt themselves. But then
I had to face the facts, they were never real, and it was just my imagination that flew the planes and moved the trains along their tracks.

I recently discovered that the playground equipment on the historic Kennedy Playground was real, but not operational. In 1964, *Ebony* magazine reported:

To some of the children the playground is a carnival and miniature world's fair all rolled into one. To others, it is a once-upon-a-time fairy tale in the 20th century. But more than this, it is a constant reminder that someone did care about them and, in addition, did something about it. The John F. Kennedy Memorial Playground is proof of that.

Clio, the Muse of History, inspires the physical renderings of sights and moments that artists witness or experience, guiding them to be faithful to both reality and imagination. She ensures that the historic events observed and portrayed by her artists are recorded as accurately as possible. She also inspires the strokes of the artist's brush, the tones and textures of the musician's melody, the emotions of the actor's tragedy and comedy, and the grace and poise of the dancer's movements. With her guidance, artists' imaginations and their recollections of history are both made real, and both realism and creativity can coexist.

Like Clio, the Leadership Muse inspires the transformation of a vision and learning into actions, plans, and substantial results. A Muse of synthesis, she brings together elements of logical analysis (generally associated with the left brain) and elements of intuition, creativity, and artistic ability (generally associated with the right brain). Warren Bennis, scholar and renowned leadership thinker, holds that the entire brain is needed for effective leadership – the right brain being where the leader *lives* with visioning, imagination, and the influence of the Leadership Muse, and the left brain being where the leader *works* and achieves accomplishments and outcomes.

For example, consider the co-leadership of Spock and McCoy on *Star Trek*. Feisty, intuitive, and empathetic, McCoy used his right-brained instinct and creativity to advise the left-brained, logical, and aloof Spock, who analyzed the information and developed plans. The crew could not have been safe or successful without the collective, whole-brained thinking of these two leaders. Together, they boldly navigated adventures and achieved the impossible, propelling themselves to other worlds long before we were able to turn the dream that *Star Trek* allowed us to imagine into reality.

Clio inspires us to use our right-brained imagination to instruct our left brains to plan and build. Without the disciplined work of the left brain, the inspiration of the right will never take form; you will imagine airplanes that never actually fly, trains that really never move, goals you dare not reach, and possibilities that don't exist. Likewise, the preparation and implementation of the left brain never brings substance to truth and beauty without the inspiration of the right; there is no picture to paint, you don't dream, infinity has an upper bound, and the impossible is unimaginable. Indeed, the power of the imagination is itself a reality we can hardly do without – in art as well as leadership. Noted visionary Ted Andrews underscores the importance of imagination:

Through creative imagination we begin to see the spiritual energies surrounding and interplaying with the physical world. What we consider imagination is a reality in some form on levels beyond the normal sensory world. With creative imagination, we create a new kind of awareness, a new kind of experience in color and form. This triggers higher forms of inspiration and intuition, giving us a higher understanding of the conditions of our lives and the spiritual energies affecting it.

Clio, who arouses the imagination through colors and forms, has often been associated with, and was perhaps often invoked by, the Dutch artist Johannes Vermeer. Though he died in obscurity and was considered crazy, Vermeer is now recognized as history's second-most renowned Dutch painter (after Rembrandt). Vermeer captured images of people where they lived, and his realistic use of color and precise representation of light make his paintings the source of centuries of admiration.

Leadership is about capturing an organization's people, processes, and technology, and painting a picture that bathes them in a fresh light. A leader with the ability to project a new vision for the future and to point out a new and challenging direction will compel an entire organization to follow him there.

Creating a compelling vision of the future requires that leaders watch for and listen to their Muses as vigilantly as Vermeer heeded Clio's influence. I am intimate with the Muse of Music, and my leadership skills owe much to her teachings. An artistic sensibility, no matter which art you practice, makes one a more creative and inspired leader; it awakens the imaginative side of the brain to inspiration. Vincent Van Gogh said, "I dream my painting, and then I paint my dream." Great leadership starts with a dream, and great achievements start with the paint needed to bring those dreams into the world.

Invoke Your Muse
Are you leading with your head and/or heart? Now, switch from heart to head, or vice versa. What would you do differently, or do more or less of? Do your actions match your words? How do you share your passion with those you lead?

Not long after my epiphany at Kennedy Playground, I got a chance to visit another place where dreams and reality, and the left and right brains, exist in marvelous tension. I took my first trip to Disneyland. Walt Disney built this place of magic, inspired by a child's dream (just like mine) and the simple notion that there should be a place where his daughters and employees' children could have fun with their parents. And from that dream and that goal, he created the happiest place in the world. As Disney put it in a 1955 speech:

To all who come to this happy place: Welcome. Disneyland is your land. Here age relives fond memories of the past, and here youth may savor the challenge and promise of the future. Disneyland is dedicated to the ideals, the dreams, and the hard facts that have created America, with the hope that it will be a source of joy and inspiration to all the world.

Whether or not your Muse is inspiring you to create a painting, write a poem, implement organizational change, win a battle, or create Disneyland, her inspiration is not without its challenges or barriers. In giving life to unbridled imagination, Walt Disney almost lost everything he owned. As the project grew in cost and scale, he had to develop creative ways to raise money, overcome construction challenges, and manage the discontent of residents who did not want the "happiest place in the world" in their backyard. As Andre Gide put it, "Art begins with resistance – at the point where resistance is overcome. No human masterpiece has ever been created without great labor." That point where resistance is overcome and labor pays off is when the right and left brains work together in perfect harmony. Walt Disney started out as a humble cartoonist, overcame barriers, took his work of art, applied some sweat and left-brained discipline, and created one of the most successful businesses ever – a testament to innovation, creativity, and hard work.

My visit to Disneyland included soaring in outer space, nearly as fast as the speed of light. I rode a train through many different frontiers and faraway lands. Traveling through time and space, I thought about the Kennedy Playground, and it came alive in my imagination once again. Clio whispered to Walt; her inspiration and his implementation made my dreams come true.

I am a mostly right-brained person in a left-brained workplace. That is not to say that my left brain is not adequate. As I child, I loved using it to translate Latin, figure out logic problems, solve differential equations, and do mathematical proofs. And as my mother always lamented, I was especially fond of useless trivia. My right-brained thinking developed as I aged. The more I trusted my intuition and empathetic skills, the better they got. Though the left-brained world in which I work doesn't usually reward this kind of thinking, the full communion of my right brain with my left has been the most significant factor in my leadership growth.

And times are changing. In *A Whole New Mind*, Dan Pink writes that right-brained thinking will soon start to rule the world; it will "suddenly grab the wheel, step on the gas, and determine where we're going and how we'll get there." This means that the left-brain's love of information and data will yield to the conceptual, big-picture thinking of the right. Thus, the right brain will spark an evolution in how we think about things.

Ultimately, I don't believe that either the right or left brain is overwhelmingly superior to the other. Both have their strengths and are necessary for effective leadership. But it's clear that there are times when our left-brain-dominated leadership thinking needs to acquiesce to the rule of the right brain. With the deluge of data and information, it is the big-picture thinking of the right brain that will help us make sense of it all. What the world needs more of is what computers can't supply – wisdom, vision, vivid imagination, and infinite creativity.

chapter 13

"Leadership is much more an art, a belief, a condition of the heart, than a set of things to do. The visible signs of artful leadership are expressed, ultimately, in its practice."

MAX DE PREE, AUTHOR OF LEADERSHIP IS AN ART

In my youth, I learned a lot from Euterpe, the Muse of Music and Lyric Poetry (also known for inspiring joy and pleasure). I began as a trumpet player but didn't have the "chops" (or the lips) for it. Perhaps it was my adolescent desire to save my lips for kissing or lipstick, but the physical challenges prevented me from getting any real joy or pleasure from playing the instrument. At age 16, I was playing in the D.C. Youth Orchestra Program's junior orchestra when I got the opportunity to audition for a temporary spot in the highly-coveted senior orchestra. They were preparing for a major concert and needed a strong, rich brass section for some works by Mahler and Stravinsky. I had no chance to make the cut on trumpet but I had always enjoyed playing around with my girlfriend's French horn and had a natural ability to make the horn *sing*. So I switched instruments. My genuine enjoyment of the music and the sound of my new French horn, coupled with my skills in music theory and sight reading, helped me retain my seat in the senior orchestra through graduation.

The next year, as a senior at Duke Ellington School of the Arts, my final exam required me to tackle a Mozart French horn concerto. Good embouchure, plus good intonation, plus *one* missed note equaled a traumatized teenage girl. Mr. Clark, our fearless leader and the head of the music department, dried my tears and told me I would have to play again next week. So I sucked it up and played. I had good embouchure and intonation, and I didn't miss the note. But I had poor phrasing from nearly hyperventilating.

I decided that music was much too stressful to pursue as a career and chose, instead, to be a … chief information officer?! (The irony doesn't escape me; perhaps it was a flash of divine madness.) So I left the stage for the arena of leadership in the public sector. These days, I don't think so much about scales, transposing, or valve oil. But then again, maybe I do, at least as it pertains to the lyrical and musical styles of a leader.

Here's what Euterpe and the French horn taught me about leadership:

SCALES AND SKILLS

A serious musician understands and practices her scales, just like the inspired leader practices her skills. Skills and scales are necessary building blocks; without them, you'll just end up with *noise* – audible or organizational. Scales are the building blocks of music. You can fit them together in many different ways to get the different outcomes you desire. There are major scales as well as the natural, harmonic, and melodic minor scales. The musician often gets to choose which scales, or keys, work best to express the feeling or statement they want to make with a particular song.

Just like there are a variety of musical scales to suit diverse purposes, there are many different expert opinions on which skills, qualities, and talents make up the building blocks of leadership. In *On Becoming a Leader*, Warren Bennis offers the notion that vision, passion, integrity, curiosity, and daring are found in most great leaders. Many leaders will have "major" strengths in some or all of these areas; others may have "minor" strengths in them. To some, it may all be "natural," and some may have "harmonic" skills that complement others on their team. And finally, leaders who have attained and subsequently lost great power may have skills that are "melodic," in that they are defined one way as they rise to power and re-defined when descending from their positions of authority. Ultimately, the organization is a symphony of players in which everyone has a job to perform, and their work must be orchestrated.

Leaders don't have to be perfect in every area to make sweet organizational music. They just have to know and play to their strengths. Consider jazz singer and trumpeter Louis Armstrong, best known for his rendition of "It's a Wonderful World." His gritty tone, coupled with rather poor enunciation, created the new musical style ("scat" singing) that made him a legend. In juxtaposing a wide range of vocal qualities, he discovered his own unique sound, one which remains a staple of almost every jazz singer's portfolio. If Armstrong had simply emulated the existing styles of his time, he wouldn't have been nearly as revolutionary or influential.

Henry Kissinger once said, "Presidents don't do great things by dwelling on their limitations, but by focusing on their possibilities." Great leaders do not focus on their weaknesses, but rather on the infinite possibilities that can be created out of their unique strengths, creativity, and circumstances. And just like *do-re-mi*, when you know the notes to sing and have the right skills, you can sing or do almost anything.

TRANSPOSITION AND TRANSFORMATION

My parents divorced when I was very young, and my father remarried many years later. I knew my stepmother for several years before I learned that she could play the piano. I was impressed and expressed my surprise to my father, the minister of music at a little, country Baptist church just outside of Richmond, Virginia. He told me, with disdain, that she played by ear – that is, she couldn't read music, didn't know her scales, and could only play in the key of C (all white keys).

Many non-professional or untrained church musicians play only in the key of C or C# (all black keys). But the songs in church hymnals are written in various key signatures. The key signature gives you the pitch on which a song will start, typically one that is comfortable for the average singer. Every now and then, when you have to play for an above-average (or below-average) singer, the key in which a song is written may not work. For example, if a soprano or tenor can't hit that high note on the word "free" in "The Star-Spangled Banner," the musician may have to transpose the song down a few *do-re-mi* steps, so that it starts out on a lower note.

Creating transformation in an organization is similar to transposition. It means taking an organization from where it is, the key in which it is written, and (or changing) it by using a diverse set of thoughts, ideas, people, and processes to create something better. Lou Gerstner, former CEO of IBM, transformed his organization in the 1990s, when the once-great technology giant was suddenly becoming increasingly less relevant. Recognizing that something needed to change, Gerstner took the company's original melody (the pride and energy behind its legacy), drew on the diverse thoughts, ideas, and processes of his people, and transformed IBM into a company that was once again relevant and viable. In the end, he turned around a culture that had become disconnected from its customers and too inwardly-focused. In addition, he shed product lines which had little promise and turned "Big Blue" back into a relevant and lean organization.

Like pianists who only play in one key, leaders who restrict their leadership efforts to what's comfortable for them, or what's tried and true in their organizations, will not be as successful at preparing and inspiring future leaders as those who are capable of transformation. Their efforts (or performances) and employees (or performers) may even fail miserably, like a singer who hits a sour note when forced to sing in the wrong key because the pianist couldn't transpose. Euterpe inspires musicians and leaders alike to be versatile, resourceful, and transformative.

VALUE AND VALVE OIL

When I was growing up, our family didn't have much money, but my mother found ways to support the needs of her three budding musicians. My sister, Loreen, played violin and clarinet, and David, my baby brother, played the euphonium and bass violin, so they needed a steady supply of rosin, strings, and reeds. I played trumpet and French horn, both of which required valve oil. Between the three of us, the costs really added up, so I helped out by saving my allowance and money earned at an after-school job where I cleaned out test tubes at an infectious diseases laboratory.

Loreen, David, our friends, and I would often walk from our home in northwest Washington, D.C., to Dale Music Store in Silver Spring, Maryland. Though it was only two-and-a-half miles away, it seemed like a cross-country trek to a teenager. In the store, we always made sure to be on our best behavior, lest we be banned and have to walk another three miles to Chuck Levin's Washington Music Center, where the older and scarier jazz musicians hung out. But I didn't care about the cost in time, wear and tear on my tennis shoes, or dollars. And if I had been forced to walk to Chuck Levin's, I would have. I cared about the value the valve oil had in keeping my instrument in tip, top shape, and that was worth the money and effort to me.

Being clear about value is equally important when it comes to successfully achieving our organizational goals. Sometimes we get caught up in how much things cost or the amount of effort needed to get them, but we neglect to quantify the value they represent. If a product, person, or service is truly imperative to reach your goal, or if having that resource might *cut* costs down the line, or if *not* having it might result in low-quality products and loss of customers, it might be worth the money. Sometimes cheap products are costly in the long run because of usability issues or maintenance needs. For example, you can buy a printer for $50, but if it runs out of ink, you might as well throw it away and buy another one.

Conversely, people often assume that things which are free have no value. In the late 1990s, I tutored in the Educational Ministry at my church. Though this service was free, many parents did not take advantage of it. Frustrated, I always felt that if we charged *something*, even $5, we would get a groundswell of support, because the service would then be *perceived* as having value.

The bottom line is that inspired leaders consider the *value*, not just the cost. They consider the big picture, not just the price tag, and make informed decisions about what they *need* to buy to make their goals a reality.

It's been more than three decades since I traded in my French horn for a career in technology. But I still hear Euterpe's voice, singing in concert with my Leadership Muse, about skills, transformation, and value. Together, they continue to teach me the song of inspired and mellifluous leadership.

chapter 14

*"When synthesizers came along, it was the first time
I thought that the two things I loved, which were
science and music, could be put together."*

HERBIE HANCOCK, AMERICAN COMPOSER, PIANIST, AND BANDLEADER

Like the nine original Muses, the Leadership Muse has her tools of the trade, which she wields with reverent and artistic skill. Musical Euterpe holds a lyre. Star-gazing Urania holds a telescope. The Muse of Information Technology (IT) stands on top of a cloud (as in cloud computing), brandishing a BlackBerry overhead in one hand, and clutching an iPad to her chest with the other, with a propeller on top of her head. Being an IT leader, I have a certain affinity for her, but she can be tremendously beneficial to any leader who listens for her voice. A leader who learns first to trust, and then to creatively use all the tools at his disposal, is a leader inspired by this 21st-century Muse.

Today, IT is *everywhere*. It is *so* everywhere that it has become cheapened as a commodity, almost to the point of seeming worthless. The proliferation and ubiquitous nature of technology, in addition to increased ease of use, makes people dismiss IT as a mere tool, rather than a skill set which requires creativity, resourcefulness, instincts, and discipline. Because we think of IT as a tool, we've lost the artistry associated with its use and mastery.

Today, technology is critical to most business initiatives. Yet, many leaders have no knowledge about how to manage IT. It's all too easy to blame the IT department or the CIO when technological limitations start getting in the way, but the smart leader will stop crying and listen to the Muse of IT. He will educate himself about IT – not necessarily in the science of the technology, but in the artistic outcomes it can produce.

Susan Cramm, author of *8 Things We Hate About IT: Moving Beyond the Frustrations to Form a New Partnership with IT*, cites a survey proving why it is important for non-IT leaders to become "IT-smart." Fifty-six percent of leaders who listen to the Muse of IT (i.e., are "IT-smart") believe that technology is "considered a competitive weapon." In other words, in the jargon of "I've got a gun and I know how to use it," they have IT and they know how to use it.

So how do you access the wisdom that the Muse of IT offers? The same as you would open yourself up to any other Muse. You familiarize yourself with the three fundamental elements of art. In addition to a little divine madness, art requires truth, beauty, and love. It is the faithful (or truthful) application of human skill and creativity that makes art beautiful and appeals to (or is loved by) those who experience it.

TRUTH. Now that anyone with a blog can be a "published" writer, what is left for the journalist to do? To coin a phrase, we live in a world where we see "information, information everywhere" but find nothing to think about. The journalist adds value by diving deep into the sea of information in which we're swimming to find the truth and meaning; in other words, he helps readers validate information and convert it into knowledge. The CIO or technology leader today finds herself in a similar position, needing to ensure that IT delivers *value* to the organization. The science of creating a blog is easy, but finding truth and knowledge in information is the journalist's art. For the leader, it is not how you do something; it is all about *why* you do it – the purpose and meaning that inspires you to analyze the data and information so that you can draw from it the truth and knowledge needed to revolutionize your organization.

BEAUTY. I recently stumbled upon Facebook photos taken by an old classmate of mine from Duke Ellington School of the Arts. I can't tell you exactly what made Francesca's photographs beautiful, but they were. The beauty was not in the tool she used, but in the results that she produced. She captured more than pixels and colors; she captured the essence – the spirit – of her subjects. I'm no art critic but I know what I like. Perhaps beauty truly is in the eye of the beholder. Similarly, the beauty in successful use of IT is not in the tools, but in the results, which can be beautiful in the eyes of those it serves. There is no beauty in pixels, code, lines of resolution, or video compression, but to those who hear the song of the Muse of IT, what these elements allow him to create is exquisite. For leaders, inspired by our Muses or blessed by grace, beauty is not measured by the output, but in whether the outcomes are perceived as *good* by those we serve, or "love."

Invoke Your Muse

Is continuous learning a way of life for you? Think of one promising piece of new technology being discussed in mainstream media. Try to find out as much as you can about it. Explore how you can use it to increase your customers' satisfaction or the quality of your work.

LOVE. Love inspires passion, which breathes life into our art – whatever form it may take and no matter how crazy it might seem to a disinterested observer. It fuels and sustains the artist through long hours in a dark room, dancing until her feet are sore, practicing his trumpet with a tired embouchure, or staring at a sentence until her eyes cross and burn. But how can you transmit a sense of passion through the sterile, objective media of IT? Sure, you can use emoticons – pictorial representations of emotions in electronic messages. But love is not conveyed by a picture of a heart, nor is happiness conveyed by a smiley face. Though IT is not an art that produces beautiful images (at least not to the untrained eye), an IT artist's passion can be conveyed by the creativity and dedication she applies to her craft. The time, attention to detail, and resourcefulness – in other words, the *love* – can produce results that make work easier and better for those she serves. And what is love, if not something that brings out the best in everyone it touches.

I have a friend who is a denizen of virtual worlds. He spent a somewhat significant amount of time *dressing* his avatar to look sexy, confident, and cool. I wonder if he realized that it was his love of this technology that breathed life into his avatar. It was the application of his programming skills, as well as his passion about the new technology and his new-found abilities, that woke up the sleeping artist in him. This love made it possible for him to devote many long hours to trial and error, learning how to develop the bits and bytes that would render an appropriate, representative image of his soul.

When it comes to IT, however, a leader must be sure that he is in love, and not just infatuated, with any particular idea, innovation, or technology. Like the sirens, who sang so sweetly that they lured sailors to certain deaths on stormy rocks, IT can be as dangerous as it is alluring for someone entranced by its potential but lacking the wisdom to distinguish lasting beauty from an exciting charade.

The siren song of the Muse of IT promises surprising benefits to the leader with a discerning ear. It is a song each leader must learn and adapt for his or her particular circumstances, always mindful of how the art of IT can work in service of truth, beauty, and love.

chapter 15

"The key here is to understand that technology isn't the ultimate power. Technology is nothing more than a side effect of rising consciousness."

MEG BLACKBURN LOSEY, SPEAKER, TEACHER, AUTHOR, AND HEALER

While the Muse of IT certainly has good intentions (to revolutionize and better the world through technological breakthroughs), it can be wise to converse with her and the Leadership Muse at the same time, because technology and society are inextricably connected. This is not a new phenomenon. Technology has ushered humankind from agrarian societies, through industrial societies, and into information societies – shaping and reshaping the way we live and work throughout the centuries. The steam engine triggered our migration to an industrial society, and *information technology* is the trigger for our ongoing migration to an information society. And of course, without humankind's infinite capacity to imagine, create, and innovate, there would be no technology.

Humankind and technology exist in a partnership in which each develops and grows as the other does. There is a point, however, at which the relationship is not so symbiotic. Clearly, we can see the economic and societal benefits of technology. But there are consequences to all inventions. The leader's job is to find the right balance and make the hard decisions about when the costs are worth the gains.

I obviously have a bias for IT. But all 21st-century leaders must consider the value and benefit that IT provides for organizations, along with the possible pitfalls. Just like with the Halloween tradition of trick or treat, we may anticipate the *treat* of technology candy, but without the requisite benefit and value, we may be *tricked* into something that proves detrimental to people and processes, and perhaps to society. Nevertheless, technology gives us a competitive advantage, and as such, leaders are tasked with weighing the possibility of being ahead of a competitor, versus the possibility of investing in something that proves to be ruinous.

The term "Luddite" has come to mean someone who hates any kind of technology. But the term was originally ascribed to a group of British textile workers who protested against the advancement of the industrial revolution. Textile factories introduced automated looms, which replaced professional weavers with cheap, unskilled labor. Historians suggest that the Luddites' disdain had more to do with the politics surrounding those advancements than with the technology itself. The invention of the weaving machine put masses of skilled artisans out of work and into poverty.

Invoke Your Muse
In executing your duties as a leader, what are the possible repercussions of missing the human elements? How do you maintain the right balance?

The Leadership Muse understands that technology can harm one group of people, like the unfortunate textile workers, while benefiting others, like factory owners and investors. Therefore, leaders who know their history and listen to the Muse know that they must be well informed and understand the limitations and possible consequences of their actions in order to avoid detrimental outcomes.

Perhaps if the leaders in the mythological lost city of Atlantis had paid closer attention to the Leadership Muse, their city would not have sunk to the ocean floor. According to legend, Atlantis, the world's most technologically-advanced society of the time, was located in the middle of the Atlantic Ocean in front of the Pillars of Hercules. Plato described it as a major naval power that had conquered many nations. Legend says that though the people of Atlantis used their technology to create a utopian society, it was the careless use of that technology, fueled by ego, that ultimately brought about their destruction. Plato's account of the events reports that Atlantis sank after a failed attempt to conquer Athens. Meg Blackburn Losey, in *The Secret History of Consciousness: Ancient Keys to Our Future Survival*, describes a theory of events based on myths and archeological evidence:

The key here is to understand that technology isn't the ultimate power. Technology is nothing more than a side effect of rising consciousness. Technology may seem to give temporary power, but as we know from ancient Egypt, the Sumerians, the stories of Lemuria and Atlantis, and even from current happenings, technology and egos simply don't mix. The combination is destructive and ultimately the demise of every power civilization that has ever been.

The Roman Empire met a similar fate. Many historians attribute the ineffective use of technology as a factor in its devastating fall. The Romans had many technological advances, particularly in weaponry, engineering, and medicine. But as they continued to expand the empire, they devoted most of their technology to building infrastructures like roads, bridges, and aqueducts in their newly-acquired territories, and neglected to produce food more efficiently so they could feed the growing population. The Romans relied heavily on the manpower afforded by slaves, but as the native people weakened and died from starvation, slaves became scarce, and work slowed dramatically. By then, it was too late.

In J.F. Cummings' book, *How to Rule the World: Lessons in Conquest for the Modern Prince*, a satirical yet strangely-instructive book, the author provides leaders with insight into why handwringing discontent must yield to proactive, rapid, strategic planning. He discusses how to thwart the effectiveness of science and technology in "your subject nation-state." In a tongue-and-cheek way, he reminds readers, "Your goal is to turn a nation-state of proactive thinkers into a band of agitated, anxiety-ridden reactionaries." So this satire suggests that doing the opposite – innovating, educating, and building capability through the proactive use of technology – will *create* proactive thinkers, a blessing for any Muse-inspired leader.

Today, with Web 2.0 technology such as Facebook, LinkedIn, and Twitter, we are able to substitute technology for personal interaction. We send text messages and e-mails in lieu of meeting in person, or even calling. We are avatars, not flesh and blood, and we have telecommuters and geographically-dispersed workers with minimal face-to-face interaction. As humans, we experience things with all of our senses. Over-use or over-reliance on technology tempts us to forget our humanity – including our sincerity, love, honesty, and mercy. These things are *felt*, not *seen* on a screen of emoticons. And technology has not (*yet*) provided the means of smelling the sweet aroma of roses or feeling the warmth of a loving embrace.

It takes the Leadership Muse, and her stores of truth, beauty, and love, to artistically and skillfully harness the power that technology offers while recognizing its limitations and keeping the well-being of *people* at the forefront. And though the focus in this chapter has been on IT, these principles apply to any leadership role. If you are a pharmaceutical executive, you don't actually produce pills; you produce the *truth* of improved health by manufacturing pharmaceuticals. If you work for a tire manufacturer, you provide a service that supports transportation, and the *beauty* of the product is in its safety and high quality. If you coached the replacement Washington Redskins – the team members and substitutes who crossed the picket line for the striking football players – you didn't call plays for scabs; you developed a team whose passion and *love* for football transformed them into Super Bowl champions.

It takes grace to do these things. Leaders must empathize, understand, and work aggressively to meet their teams where they are and encourage them to be brilliant for a common cause. This is why the ancient Muses were always closely allied with the Graces. They provided the inspiration while the Graces ensured pleasing outcomes.

chapter 16

"Never underestimate the power of free food. I can't offer any rational explanation, but for geeks, even those making sizeable incomes, free food offers major support to motivation development, far more than an equivalent amount of cash."

**PAUL GLEN, AUTHOR OF LEADING GEEKS:
HOW TO MANAGE AND LEAD PEOPLE WHO DELIVER TECHNOLOGY**

One of my favorite old TV shows is *The Twilight Zone*. The classic version, narrated by Rod Serling, is no longer on the air, but remembering some of the twisted scenarios always makes me either chuckle to myself or ponder some of the hidden messages and meanings. The show's premise required the viewer to believe in the impossible for a few moments and to follow the narrator on a journey to a place of unconventional thinking. There was one episode entitled "To Serve Man," which was about seemingly-friendly, humble, and servile aliens from outer space. But it turned out that they really wanted to serve man . . . for dinner.

Leaders are often exhorted to "serve" those we lead. No, we don't eat our followers alive, but *The Twilight Zone's* play on words made me think – what does "to serve" really mean in the leadership context? Do we assist our followers or do we consume them? Do we help them grow and leave them better than they were, or do we just leave them? The narrator's words present a grim reality and make it sound as if it could happen to anyone:

These are the recollections of one Michael Chambers, with appropriate flashbacks and soliloquy. Or more simply stated, the evolution of man, the cycle of going from dust to dessert, the metamorphosis from being the ruler of a planet to an ingredient in someone's soup. It's tonight's bill of fare on The Twilight Zone.

While the aliens probably did not struggle over the morality of eating earthlings, for human leaders, the question of how to serve poses a dilemma. The flourishing leader should not treat those she leads as mere tasty morsels, to be feasted upon as one of the many consumable ingredients contributing to her many accomplishments. Followers are people, not commodities or resources to be managed.

The distinction between these two approaches – whether followers are resources to be utilized or a group to be served – lies in the question: Who is serving whom? Employees provide us with a service in exchange for rewards, recognition, and self-actualization. If we want to keep them happy, productive, and inspired, we must also serve them respect, care, trust, gratitude, and consideration for the good work they do for us.

For example, when I needed to fill a key leadership position (my second in command), I thought about a particular employee who worked for me (I'll call him William). I was at my wit's end, and I believed William could be my salvation. But to do this – to serve me – he would have to relocate across the country to D.C. He was not able to move his entire family, so he would have to be away from them and endure the financial hardship of maintaining two households while commuting coast-to-coast. He was also in the middle of implementing much-needed organizational changes in one of our field locations. Accepting this position would mean leaving an organization he had just started to build, disrupting his career and family, and never actualizing his leadership vision.

I asked him to take the assignment in D.C., and he agreed. However, just because people *will* do anything for you doesn't mean that you should *ask* them to sacrifice for you, especially something life-changing, without first thinking about them as people. How many men and women have given their lives (literally and metaphorically) when called to serve a leader? But how many leaders have been willing to give their lives when called to serve the people who follow them? In comparing the two scenarios, I bet we would find that the former far outnumbers the latter.

If we have people willing to sacrifice their lives for us — whether that means moving, commuting, or working every weekend — it's only fair to consider what we would be willing to sacrifice for them. William, for example, was willing to sacrifice his needs for mine. I spent a lot of time questioning whether I would be serving him by asking him to serve me. And when I evaluated the situation with empathy for him, I rescinded my request and released him from his agreement.

Invoke Your Muse

When you lead someone who will sacrifice for you, what will you sacrifice for his or her sake? Have you ever done this? Can you think of opportunities right now to do this?

Nelson Mandela sacrificed nearly three decades of his personal freedom in a lonely prison cell to fight apartheid. He was very clear about who he served and what his followers needed from him. He was willing to sacrifice everything for them, and undoubtedly many of his followers would have done the same for him. A leader who practices this type of reciprocal respect and gratitude for those who serve him becomes a powerful Muse for future generations.

As leaders, we like to say that people are our first priority. But do we actually *do* anything to live up to this lofty statement? Saying it is one thing, but acting on it is another. The Leadership Muse knows that it is important to demonstrate gratitude. This does not mean giving our employees everything they want, but it does mean giving them everything they need – and maybe a little something extra here and there to show appreciation.

As an IT leader, I am lucky to lead and serve those who focus most of their lives on technology. These people are most commonly and endearingly known as "geeks." And we should all give thanks to our geeks. They work long hours with little sleep, concentrate on problems until they are solved, and ask for very little in return… except Red Bull and pizza!

In *Leading Geeks: How to Manage and Lead People Who Deliver Technology*, Paul Glen suggests several ways to motivate geeks. One strategy is to organize collections of tasks into projects as often as possible. No one likes working day-in and day-out on tasks with no objectives and no end. Creating projects (when appropriate) helps team members focus energy on specific outcomes and fosters an environment of accomplishment.

Glen also suggests bringing food for your geeks (and I bet this one would work with "normal" workers as well). I recall one night during my happier days as a systems programmer (a.k.a., geek) when I got a call at home from my boss around 7:00 p.m. When she asked what I was doing, I thought, "Uh-oh." To her, I said, "I'm watching *Wheel of Fortune*. What's up?" She asked if I could come into the office and help her; there was a little problem. Well, after almost two days and nights of not leaving the office, napping on the floor using my purse for a pillow, and getting very little sleep, we finally fixed the "little" problem.

On the second day, after we had been up all night, her boss came in at lunchtime with food! Potato salad and fried chicken was the fuel needed to keep our engines running for another 24 hours. That was nearly 25 years ago, but I still remember how that food tasted and how it sustained me through another sleepless night. We found the problem and had to accurately reconstruct the data on the failed devices. The work was tedious and time-consuming, but fueled with food that was high in fats and carbohydrates and low in nutritional value, we stayed awake and alert for another 24 hours, due in no small part to being supported by a boss who at least knew what we were going through. He thought enough of us to bring in some tasty morsels. And though he was a healthy eater, he knew what kind of food nerdy, propeller-heads love. He didn't simply suck us dry or consume us for what we were worth and for what we could do; instead, he knew enough to serve us and *feed* us, metaphorically and literally.

chapter 17

*"The true leader serves. Serves people. Serves their best interests,
and in doing so will not always be popular, may not always impress.
But because true leaders are motivated by loving concern rather
than a desire for personal glory, they are willing to pay the price."*

EUGENE B. HABECKER IN THE OTHER SIDE OF LEADERSHIP

Being a supportive and inspiring leader requires more than bringing in cold chicken and leftover potato salad, though that always goes over big. We must also be prepared to feed those we serve with the resources we are given, often before we feed ourselves. Leadership often means sacrifice – not just giving to others, but living for others.

A colleague of mine, forgetting the value of self-sacrifice, once made a misstep that cost her a job. Her new boss complained about the printers issued by her IT department, reporting that when he asked his secretary to print something for him, it took too long. My friend, seeking to impress him, brought a new color, laser printer for him – and one for herself while she was at it – leaving his secretary with the old, slow printer. Her boss was angry about this and mumbled something about how he'd rather have new boots for his soldiers than a new horse for himself.

After an escalating series of similar missteps, he finally removed her from the position. She didn't understand why, so she asked me. I explained that, in service to others, she should have first made sure the secretary had a fast, high-quality printer; in service to herself, she sought to impress her new boss with her bountiful resources and to accessorize her ego with the fanciest and most expensive printer in the organization. Service and sacrifice means not thinking about what success means to our egos, but about what success means to the people we serve.

In Greek mythology, (not "Geek" mythology – that's a completely different book), the cornucopia was associated with magical powers. Those who possessed the cornucopia got anything they wished for. Later, this horn of plenty was associated with food and abundance – a receptacle that refilled itself as soon as it was empty. Good, resourceful leaders possess the equivalent of a cornucopia, and the best leaders know how to use it to make sure no one in their spheres of influence goes without. The significance here is two-fold:

FIRST, YOU MUST WISH FOR SOMETHING. For leaders, this means having a vision, being able to communicate that dream or goal in an inspiring way, and providing a path people want to follow. The title character on the TV sitcom *I Dream of Jeannie* once explained that all she did was "think and blink" and then her magic happened. I always get frustrated when we go through annual strategic-planning processes to define vision and we get hung up on words. Leadership vision is not a statement. It is about helping people see that they are part of something big. It inspires loyalty and commitment and motivates our teams to stretch and grow. Leaders *think* about their vision and then they *blink* it into reality with substantive actions and plans.

EVERY LEADER HAS A CORNUCOPIA TO FILL. Even before you make your wish, you must have a plan for what you will do with the food and goodness your cornucopia will produce, because once it fills, you will end up with rot and waste if you aren't prepared to give back. This is the essence of *servant-leadership*. In his book *Think and Grow Rich*, Napoleon Hill decries the backlash of the machine age as it reduces leaders to think of their followers as mere machines. When there is true understanding of the connection between the worker's state of mind and the organization's output and production, a leader can accomplish more than he ever thought possible. Many successful industrialists and businessmen, including Charles Schwab, accumulated wealth by giving, by sharing the contents of their cornucopias *before* they tasted the fruits of their own labor. Every successful leader needs followers to help him reap the abundance of plans realized, outcomes achieved, and visions actualized. As these rewards are harvested, the servant-leader must be prepared to give back in humble gratitude.

The servant-leader believes in responding to the needs of others before her own and she does the work necessary to identify those needs – even if that requires stepping into their shoes. In *Divine Moments for Leaders*, Ronald Beers writes about the practice of "downward mobility" (or being willing to perform the most menial tasks) as a way to grow as a leader. CBS's reality show *Undercover Boss* takes this theory to a literal level by bringing executives out of their corner offices and placing them in front-line jobs in their organizations. Working alongside their employees while hiding their true identities, they see how their decisions affect the people who work for them and get a true picture of the inner-workings of their companies – the good, the bad, and the ugly. The profound effect on these leaders is striking. They come away with life-changing lessons in humility that transform the essence of their leadership. On one episode, Larry O'Donnell, chief operating officer of the $13-billion-dollar company Waste Management, poses as a garbage collector and gains a better understanding of how hard his employees work, how devastating poor corporate communications can be on morale, and the outcome of poorly-crafted policies.

I once knew a pastor who would always say, "I wish I didn't know these things!" Once you know right from wrong, he argued, you have the responsibility to choose "right." And once you know, you *have* to do something ... *and* it has to be the right thing. It might be theoretically better (or at least easier) not to know, because after you are more aware of yourself and others, you become more accountable. As they say, to whom much is given, much is expected. But the benefits to leaders willing to embrace the work of their followers, and to truly know the effects of every decision they make all the way down the line, are immeasurable and will keep their cornucopias overflowing.

The knowledge that breeds responsibility will come from diverse sources. This diversity of perspectives and opinions may breed creative conflicts. If you ask for perspectives, be prepared to actually listen and try to understand, and to practice grace for yourself and others.

Most executives leave the show *Undercover Boss* understanding that their leadership could use a bit of servitude – for the sake of their workers and for the sake of what low morale can do to their bottom lines. Robert Greenleaf, founder of the Greenleaf Center for Servant Leadership, elaborates on this management concept in his essay, "Servant as Leader." He explains:

[Leadership] begins with the natural feeling that one wants to serve, to serve first. Then conscious choice brings one to aspire to lead. The best test is: do those served grow as persons; do they, while being served, become healthier, wiser, freer, more autonomous, more likely themselves to become servants? And, what is the effect on the least privileged in society; will they benefit or at least, not be further deprived?

Greenleaf says that the truly great leader is, at heart, a servant first. He sacrifices himself for the needs of those he serves. Mother Teresa was such a servant. She believed that for "a sacrifice to be real, it must cost, must hurt, [and we] must empty ourselves." As she once explained, "The fruit of silence is prayer, the fruit of prayer is faith, the fruit of faith is love, the fruit of love is service, and the fruit of service is peace." And in her lifetime, she led a ministry that served millions.

This doesn't mean that leaders need to be like Mother Teresa or even have the riches of a Bill Gates or a Rockefeller. In their book, *The Power of Half,* Hannah and Kevin Salwen describe how selling their house and donating half the proceeds ($800,000) to villages in Ghana changed their lives. In making a difference for others, they experienced the pleasant but unintended consequence of changing their own lives. They also donated their time and manpower, moving to an environment very different from theirs – across an ocean and in another continent. But the more they learned about the people they were serving, the more they came to understand themselves. And their experiment inspired many others to start their own "half" projects. Ultimately, an effective leader must also be able to assume the role of follower.

Invoke Your Muse

Work on developing servant-leadership habits. Journal about what you could do and hold yourself accountable for doing something daily for at least 21 days. For example, you could bring coffee for your administrative staff, buy a bottle of cold water for the security guard standing in the heat, or give candy to your computer technician. How would such random acts of servant-leadership change you? How would it change your followers?

Leaders learn about improving themselves and others by giving – whether it is half an hour, half the profits, or half a pizza. The lesson of the cornucopia, however, goes deeper than free food. The courageous servant-leader dares to distribute the full power of her cornucopia; she gives away recognition and saves none for herself; and she helps others see beyond their self-limitations to accomplish more than they ever imagined. She is true to herself and others, is both passionate and humble about the good work she does, and sincerely loves those she serves (often those who also serve her). Thanks to her acts of grace, there is always enough to feed the multitude.

chapter 18

"It is better to lead from behind and to put others in front,
especially when you celebrate victory when nice things occur.
You take the front line when there is danger.
Then people will appreciate your leadership."

NELSON MANDELA

In ancient Greek mythology, the Graces were the goddesses of joy, charm, and beauty. Aglaia, Euphrosyne, and Thaleia – the daughters of Zeus and the nymph Eurynome – are treated as a group, always depicted in a circle of three. Described as attendants in service to others, including other divinities, they personify Aaron Atsma's concept that "real joy exists only in circles where the individual gives up his own self and makes it his main object to afford pleasure to others."

The leadership lesson the Graces teach is a divine paradox. As Atsma puts it, "The less beauty is ambitious to rule, the greater is its victory; and the less homage it demands, the more freely it is paid." This is the spirit of the servant-leader. The word "grace" means undeserved or unearned favor. Leaders inspired by the Graces show favor to their followers, not because they are valuable human resources to manage, or because the Graces want to receive appreciation and esteem, but because this divine leadership style yields miraculous results.

The Graces were almost always depicted as full-figured and naked, with the truth of their unashamed beauty out there for all to see. Servant-leaders are equally courageous in their willingness to operate and lead transparently. Sure, such vulnerability could mean occasionally exposing oneself in non-complimentary ways, but people will forgive imperfect leaders who are brave enough to be honest. After all, none of us are perfect.

However, leaders who are reluctant to being vulnerable, or who commit to hiding their true selves, should consider asking themselves what their secrecy exposes about them as leaders. And while they may think they are hiding their faults, they are wrong. Everyone knows that everyone makes mistakes. Leaders will occasionally make some, and if they don't take it on the chin when they do, they risk being seen as dishonest. In hiding behind masks of infallibility, they will not be able to earn the followership needed for critical successes. Ironically, the courage to be vulnerable and imperfect helps us overcome the risks associated with self-exposure.

Invoke Your Muse

Have you ever worked for a real jerk? Are you currently working for someone who is unpleasant and/or offensive? Think of the strategies you used (or can use) to look beyond his/her obnoxious personality and do your job. Did you see the good in that jerk? How?

In addition to being courageously honest, the Graces also inspire leaders to be self aware – to know the difference between their true *selves* and the masks that "self" tends to hide behind. Being self-aware means knowing your own strengths and weaknesses so that you can use or develop them appropriately. And knowing your personality and preferences can help you navigate through difficult situations – particularly with people who are different from you.

The self-aware leader surrounds himself with people who will tell him the truth – even when it is unpleasant. We can all learn something from the absolutely unaware emperor who decided to don a transparent wardrobe. Everyone told him how great his new threads were, allowing him to parade naked through town, until a courageous follower finally told him that he wasn't wearing clothes. The modern-day emperor will likewise encounter people with varying levels of sincerity, including those who tell him that he's doing a heck-of-a-job, even when he isn't. Grace-full leaders seek out and serve courageous followers who will tell them when they are, in fact, wearing no clothes. You will find these truthful followers when you build a diverse team – a team that complements your strengths and mitigates your weaknesses. They will bring different perspectives and experiences to your situation. You will find them in technical areas that are dissimilar to your own. In short, these followers may not look like you, act like you, or think like you, and fortunately for any exposed emperors, they won't dress like you.

The self-aware leader must, above all, have high emotional intelligence and be capable of honest self-examination. Even if a leader falls victim to a blind spot, she must have the courage to own up to it, much like the Emperor in the 1987 movie rendition of the tale, who confessed:

I, as Emperor, was OVERPOWERINGLY stupid. I, as Emperor, was more stupid than you all, because I was responsible for all this stupidity!

Finally, Grace-full leadership demands that we look beyond the faults of those we lead and serve them responsibly, with patience, compassion, and consideration. In serving others with love, the servant-leader helps them see the beauty inside themselves.

Giving each other and ourselves the grace to be honest but non-judgmental, to forgive mistakes while still encouraging excellence, and to be aware with kindness – all of this goes a long way in life and in leadership. I was fortunate to learn this from a Grace-full leader early in my career. As a young programmer, my boss allowed me to operate independently. When I made mistakes that crashed the system, she took the blame for it and helped me learn from these errors so I could grow into an expert technician. She regularly assigned me tasks beyond my ability. However, she made sure I was comfortable and trained and had all the tools I needed to grow, learn, and contribute to the mission of the organization.

One historical leader, aptly named Grace, provides a lesson in Grace-full leadership. Though her name isn't as recognizable as Orville and Wilbur Wright, Thomas Edison, or Benjamin Franklin, Grace Hopper's leadership as an inventor and innovator changed history. She made it possible for the average person to program a computer, taking the mystery and marvel of the digital computing machine out of the laboratory and putting it out into the world.

The power of Grace Hopper's leadership was in her followership. Following the call to serve her country led her to serve a leader for whom she had profound respect and faith. She translated this conviction and belief into words and actions that empowered both her crew and a community of others. She gave away power to her followers and never took credit for their work. As she once put it, "Leadership is a two-way street, loyalty up and loyalty down. Respect for one's superiors; care for one's crew."

This tiny woman walked in a giant, unwelcoming world. She stood 5-feet, 6-inches tall and weighed about 105 pounds, a woman against the "computer" (at that time, a machine that was 51 feet long, eight feet tall, two feet deep, and 10,000 pounds). But she conquered this intimidating colossus by creating the capability to translate common, English-like commands into the machine's arcane mathematical language.

A mathematician born in a time when very few women went to college and even fewer obtained advanced degrees in the sciences, Hopper was one of only 396 Americans to receive an advanced degree between 1930 and 1934, and the first woman to receive a degree in mathematics from Yale. After school, she obtained a teaching position at Vassar College. Her teaching style mirrored her learning style. She loved studying diverse subjects and audited many courses while she taught. Then she'd use what she learned to present information in ways that related and appealed to a variety of people.

PHOTO COURTESY OF JAMES DEAN

FRED FRIENDLY ATTEMPTING TO TALK OVER GRACE HOPPER WITH JIM DEAN IN 1989.

When Pearl Harbor was attacked in 1941, Hopper left her tenured position at Vassar to join the Women Accepted for Emergency Volunteer Service (WAVES), which assigned her to work in the Harvard Computation Laboratory, programming one of the world's first computers. She worked under the challenging leadership of Commander Howard

Aiken – a demanding, autocratic man who did not appreciate being given a woman to help him. But she looked beyond his rough exterior and abrasive personality and became very loyal and invaluable to him.

Hopper was skilled at bringing diverse people together and finding the common, fertile ground where the whole of their contributions was greater than the sum of what they could offer as individuals. She overcame technical challenges and gender bias to gain the respect of those she led and those she served. During the war, it was tremendously challenging to find food and supplies. Nevertheless, she found creative ways to get her early geeks the things that they needed. Reflecting on her service and contributions, Commander Aiken once said, "Grace was a good man."

Hopper's contributions were not without personal sacrifice. Her own special type of *madness* drove her decision to serve, which brought about the end of her marriage, leaving her childless and divorced during an era when women were defined by their roles as wives and mothers. Furthermore, the stress of her long hours and difficult work environment caused periodic bouts of depression and alcoholism.

Later in her career, she would write several uncredited papers providing instruction on the use of automatic programming, which suddenly made computers practical and cost-effective for efficiently solving business problems. The new computers were powerful, but the cost to program these giants was tremendous. Her work made it possible to provide instructions to a computer in English-like commands and not numerical machine codes, meaning that a high-school graduate could give instructions to these behemoths, rather than a limited set of Ph.D. mathematicians.

In 1959, Hopper laid the foundation for the creation of the Committee on Data Systems and Languages (CODASYL), bringing together 40 representatives from seven government agencies, 11 companies, and 10 computer manufacturers to create a common business language – COBOL, the language anyone over age 30 had to learn in computer programming classes.

It's hard to imagine the impact of Hopper's work today, when computer programming is so much a part of our lives that we take it for granted. But imagine if there was no Facebook, or a even world without the technology to print the book you are reading. Someone wrote computer programs to create Facebook, and someone wrote computer programs to print this book. And Grace Hopper invented the "art" of computer programming, which enabled these feats. True to her namesakes, the Graces, she made her art accessible to everyone – and what a cornucopia that turned out to be! Today's open-source approach to collaboration and the development of the Internet owes a great deal to her legacy. The open-source approach gives software code away for free, making it available to the masses, who offer suggestions for enhancements in return. How Grace-like! Hopper was once quoted as saying, "To me, programming is more than an important, practical art. It is also a gigantic undertaking in the foundations of knowledge."

While something as arcane as computer programming might not seem very artistic to many people, for those inspired by the Muse of IT, there is no question that Grace Hopper invented her own art form. In *The Art in Computer Programming*, Andrew Hunt and David Thomas explain the similarities between creating a work of art and developing a computer program. Painters start with a blank canvas and must know when to stop so they don't ruin the artwork with too much paint. Like novelists and painters, computer programmers get writer's block and often have a hard time getting to the point called "done." A programmer who does not know when to stop ends up with a product that has too many features and too little usability. The programmer-artist must also satisfy the sponsor who commissioned the work. And customer satisfaction, which is analogous to "beauty" in art, is in the eye of the beholder, or in programming language, the end-user.

Grace Hopper's innovations accomplished the Muse's work of engendering artists and giving them tools to revolutionize the art-form itself.

She created a safe environment for young, up-and-coming programmers and nurtured their ability to innovate and create. Her goal was to empower people as a collective, rather than herself as an individual. So she brought together a diverse team to create and design together, believing that ideas from the group would be stronger than hers alone. By bringing people together, understanding the needs of those she led, and subordinating her own glory and needs, this Grace left a giant footprint on the world.

I had the pleasure of meeting Hopper several times and I know people who interacted with her personally. She was feisty, irreverent, and clearly able to hold her own, even in the presence of giants. In the ceremony where she was promoted to commodore, her nephew related a story about how she had ordered President Reagan around. Reagan reported to be tickled with this, and the two had a natural affinity for each other. She died in 1992, but I still think of her when I hear her Muse, the Muse of IT, whispering inspiring, sassy, and irreverent songs in my ear.

chapter 19

THE EVERYDAY MUSE

*"Gracefulness has been defined to be the outward
expression of the inward harmony of the soul."*

WILLIAM HAZLITT, BRITISH AUTHOR

The Greeks saw the Graces as goddesses of charm, beauty, nature, human creativity, and fertility. They were special favorites of Aphrodite and Eros, the divinities of love. And they worked closely with the Muses, with whom they sang on Mount Olympus, also inspiring artists to create beautiful works of art.

When we meet leaders who are artists, who practice their professions with skill and grace, we find ourselves in the presence of inspiring individuals even more remarkable than these ancient mystical beings, because these leaders are so very human. And these extraordinary leaders don't just congregate in C-suites at *Fortune* 500 companies. They also run small businesses, lead nonprofit organizations, or even cut hair.

Peggy, my hairdresser, could be one of the Graces, or a Muse in a human disguise. She learned her work ethic on a farm in what used to be rural Clinton, Maryland. When the farms disappeared and the D.C. suburbs began to expand, Peggy started her own business – Peggy's Beauty World.

When I visit her shop, she always asks me about how things are going at work and what my job is like. One day, as she stood over my head, she confessed that she probably wouldn't understand my job because, after all, she's "just a hairdresser." Startled, I turned to look at her. Peeking around her comb, I explained to her just how much she *already* understood about being a successful business leader. Here are some lessons from this beautiful, very-human Grace.

CUSTOMER SERVICE AND BEAUTY

After many successful years, Peggy sold her business and established a small, licensed shop in her home so she could keep a handful of her most faithful clients and offer them flexible, personalized service. I have been to see her at 10:00 p.m. on a Sunday night, at 5:00 a.m. on a Monday morning before work, a few hours before I had to leave town, and even in 911-hair emergencies. If you don't like your hair, she will do it again. She's even been known to make house calls for home-bound clients. I've often asked her how business is doing during these difficult financial times. It's no surprise that she continues to thrive.

Mark Cummuta, in a CIO.com blog called "How to Avoid a Layoff," advises leaders to focus on customer service to get through difficult financial times without needing to downsize. By doing so, their customers become their strongest advocates. He writes:

No matter what job or position you have, you always have customers — whether they be internal managers, peers, business units, branch offices, downstream partners, QA teams, PMOs, sales teams, etc. – that rely on what you produce. They may not even know it, but in today's economic turmoil, it's to your benefit to know who they are and to make sure they know what you can and do, in fact, do for them!

Grace-full leaders like Peggy love what they do and those for whom they do it. The quality of Peggy's customer service speaks to the love she holds for those she serves, and they return the favor.

LEADING AND MANAGING IN TRUTH AND AUTHENTICITY

As a beauty shop owner, Peggy has hired, trained, and mentored many young women. She has employed a diverse set of people, from urban divas to seasoned professionals. She has hired and fired, and dealt with tears, fears, and jeers. Yet, through all of this, she maintained a business known for ethical, family-oriented, high-quality services.

Invoke Your Muse

Think of someone who, in his or her everyday life and work, is an artist who inspires and makes magic just by practicing what he or she loves. It could be your dog trainer, the receptionist at your dentist office, or the lady next door who makes wedding cakes. Describe this person and what makes him or her inspirational.

One of the leader's greatest challenges is figuring out how to motivate her employees. Peggy once had to coach an employee on how to handle a customer who was not happy with the hair weave she'd just gotten. Getting a weave is an expensive and time-consuming process where a beautician takes strips of hair and meticulously sews them, with a special needle and thread, to her client's hair. If a weave is too tight, it is uncomfortable; if it's too loose, it pulls the hair and looks unsightly. This customer was not satisfied with this expensive service, and the young beautician was nearly in tears at the prospect of returning so much money. But Peggy showed her how to work through it with a few extra strands of hair, some strategic cuts, and a bottle of semi-permanent color. The happy customer would come back soon for more color and another cut, and Peggy's wise, compassionate edits to the young beautician's work ensured her loyalty and dedication to her employer.

THE POWER OF PASSION

Peggy is passionate about hair so she absolutely loves her job. In her youth, when she was trying to figure out what to do for a living, her mother admonished her, insisting the decision was obvious: She loved doing hair. Before Peggy sold her business, she was extremely busy and had to be on her feet for nearly 10 hours at a time. But she was always smiling at the end of the day. "You never get tired when you are doing something you love," she told me. "It gives you energy." I could almost hear the Muses applauding, honoring the work of this humble artist, a hairdresser in the suburbs of Washington, D.C.

Peggy is proof that passion and hard work are keys to success. I couldn't believe she told me that she was "just a hairdresser." Every two weeks, this tenth Muse, this noble Grace, does so much more than turn the unwashable bird's nest on top of my head into pretty curls; she also gives me a little bit of inspiration.

part three
Appearances of My Muse

chapter 20

WISDOM OF THE WING

"Birds have often been considered the symbols of the soul.
Their ability to fly reflects the ability within us to rise to new
awareness, bridging the earth and the heavens. As totems, birds
each have their own peculiar characteristics, but they can all be
used to stimulate greater flights of hope, inspiration and ideas."

TED ANDREWS, AUTHOR OF ANIMAL-SPEAK:
THE SPIRITUAL & MAGICAL POWERS OF CREATURES GREAT & SMALL

One dream shared by generations of humans – from the first moment of self-consciousness when we realized our physical limitations (and then tried to transcend them) – is the dream of flight. This is probably why wings and birds have always been symbols of spirituality and mysticism. In art, the Muses were always represented with wings. Similarly, wings are associated with the heavenly truth of angels and other divine messengers.

Birds have always been an inspiration and a source of awe for mankind, and without what we know of them, we human beings might still be grounded. Inspired by birds, Daedalus, the mythological inventor imprisoned on the island of Crete because the gods thought he was too smart, tried to escape by fashioning two sets of wings out of wax and feathers – one for himself and one for his son, Icarus. The story ends in tragedy, with Icarus flying too close to the sun, melting the wax, and falling to his death in the sea. But while Icarus is remembered as foolish, his father's sense of invention is revered. Ancient depictions of Daedalus always show him with wings – symbolizing his ingenuity and craftiness.

That our human ancestors looked to the birds for wisdom is evident in the story of Daedalus and many other stories and legends – as well as in history. One of my favorite places to visit is Kitty Hawk, N.C. I love this

PHOTO COURTESY OF LISA T. WATSON

MY NIECE, ALYSSA, READY FOR TAKE-OFF ON A SAND DUNE IN KITTY HAWK AS SHE PONDERS HER AUNT'S DREAM OF FLYING.

quiet beach town with its warm, ocean breeze. The restaurants have cool names with alliteration like Awful Arthur's, Bad Barracuda, Coastal Cravings, and Dirty Dick's. Many folks travel to this sleepy, coastal spot to get away from it all and forget about the day-to-day stresses of life. For me, it has always been a place of renewal. One of my best vacations was when my husband, Doug, and I celebrated our fifth wedding anniversary in Kitty Hawk. We stayed up all night watching movies, caught up with an entire season of the TV show *24*, and slept away most of the days. On another occasion, I was driving down to North Carolina when I received a call from my new boss telling me that I was getting promoted. A few days of celebration and relaxation followed.

Perhaps the real reason I love Kitty Hawk is because this enchanted place where dreams blow in on a damp breeze across the Atlantic Ocean is the birth-place of human flight – where the Wright Brothers invented and demonstrated the technology that gave wings to mankind.

Orville and Wilbur Wright didn't finish high school, but they were re-sourceful and well-read. They started a printing business with a printing press they built from recycled parts and later opened a bicycle-repair shop. Then they became fascinated, perhaps attending to the coaxing of their Muses, with the less-traveled road to *flight* – a successful path that would ultimately require determination, ingenuity, and faith. In early versions of their flying machine, they used their own bodies to control the shape and configuration of the wings. By moving their heads and hips, they could control the mech-anisms which moved the wings. In their analysis, they theorized:

...twisting the wings so as to present their ends to the wind at different an-gles is a more prompt and efficient way of maintaining lateral equilibrium than that employed in shifting the body of the operator of the machine.

They risked their lives to prove that man could fly in a self-powered contraption made of spruce. Each early "landing" was actually a crash that often resulted in bumps and bruises for the inventors. Yet, with the madness of their convictions driving them to push forward, they finally made a reality of Daedalus' vision.

Think of how Orville and Wilbur must have studied the seagulls and herons of the southern east coast! What they learned from birds taught them the power of flight. Because of their ability to fly, birds have always been considered to have special access to the gods and the supernatural powers that shape our world. My friend, David the Desert Horseman (whom you will read more about in a few chapters), believes, as do many Native Americans, that people have animal spirit guides or totems. The animal spirit guides enter and leave our lives depending on where we are in our journeys or what we need at any particular time. Animal totems, on the other hand, stay with us for life, offering power and wisdom to those who acknowledge and respect them. David thinks mine might be the hummingbird, the eagle, and the owl. And so, following the promptings of my Muse, I have branched out beyond the wax and feathers of Daedalus and the engineering of the brothers of flight to study these heavenly ambassadors and sages for what they have to teach me.

Ted Andrews, in *Animal-Speak: The Spiritual & Magical Powers of Creatures Great and Small*, describes how learning to speak to and listen to animals can increase our human potential. When we connect with animals in this Muse-like way:

They become our teachers, our friends, and our companions. They show us the true majesty of life itself. They restore our forgotten childlike wonder at the world, and they reawaken our lost belief in magic, dreams, and possibilities.

Whether or not we believe in such magic, we can learn a lot from the animal world. Animals are experts at survival and adaptation. Some are great nurturers and protectors, and others are full of strength, courage, and playfulness. I am certain that birds served as the Muses of Flight for Orville and Wilbur, motivating them to endure countless bumps and bruises so that humankind could finally have wings. Perhaps the characteristics of my own avian spirit guides –which we'll explore in the next few chapters – can offer valuable insight into the lessons of the Leadership Muse.

Chapter 21

From scarlet to powdered gold,
to blazing yellow,
to the rare
ashen emerald,
to the orange and black velvet
of your shimmering corselet,
out to the tip
that like
an amber thorn
begins you,
small, superlative being,
you are a miracle,
and you blaze

PABLO NERUDA, FROM "ODE TO THE HUMMINGBIRD"

In St. Thomas, another of my favorite places, the gentle, tropical breeze welcomes travelers into a strong, diverse culture. Evidence of many years of colonial occupation is visible in the architecture, as well as the influences of Dutch, Caribbean, African and decidedly-American traditions. Luxurious beaches with clear, blue waters are bordered by a magnificent array of colorful plants and flowers. Many of these plants, like hibiscus and bougainvillea, are familiar to me from my grandmother's garden. Other plants, like the prickly cactus, denizen of the desert, are more startling to behold, as they create their own oasis amid the tropics.

On a tour of St. Thomas with my friend, Stephanie, and her sister, Ann, where we got the opportunity to buy things we didn't want at very low prices and admire the natural beauty of the island, my Muse visited me in the form of one of my animal totems. I stood outside of our bus, waiting somewhat patiently for the driver to return. Being a D.C. diva, I was not especially appreciative of the opportunity to commune with nature and her animals. It didn't help that Stephanie was still recovering from the trauma of being attacked by a vicious swarm of butterflies that we were quite sure, at first, were killer bees. (The reader must understand here that we are city girls and tend to freak out when something flies too close to our hair.) Ann, who was celebrating her 70th birthday, thought sitting down in the air-conditioned, deluxe motor coach would be a more desirable option at that moment. But we stood patiently in the sun fanning ourselves, on guard for brutal butterflies, carnivorous cacti, or anything else that might bring harm to us. Yes, we were supposed to rest and renew while communing with nature, but at this moment, it was all about survival and souvenirs.

As we waited, I began to share Ann's desire to sit. I found a nice, shady spot free of bugs and rested there. Suddenly, there was some commotion in the group; a gigantic was gecko teasing us. Someone got its attention, and it crossed the road (presumably to get to the other side). I was grateful that this city girl had escaped a perilous brush with a gecko. As I stood to regain my composure, I felt something strange, sort of like someone was watching me.

It was too close to see, really, hovering just inside the area where my eyes could focus. I stepped back a bit. At first, I wasn't sure what it was. I thought my hair was about to be ravaged by one of those gigantic killer bees Stephanie warned me about. Yet, I didn't lose my composure and respond in my usual fashion (swatting, screaming, and running). Instead,

I stayed still, and as my vision cleared, I recognized the beautiful blue, yellow, and green winged creature hovering in front of my eyes as a hummingbird. I figured this flying rainbow would flit away soon, but it didn't. It just hovered there, suspended in the air, and spoke to me for what seemed like an eternity.

Oh my, I was missing a photo opportunity. The hummingbird flirted with me as I pulled out my camera and turned it on. The distinctive sound of the digital camera booting up caused my new friend to retreat to a safe but still-enticing distance. The spell was broken.

In Native-American mythology, the tiny hummingbird is powerfully significant. The Hopi and Zuni cast the hummingbird as the hero of humankind. According to their legends, in times of drought, it intervened on behalf of humans, convincing the gods to send rain. For this reason, the hummingbird is thought to have a special relationship with the rain gods so that it knows where deep sources of water are located and how to mediate between the divine and human worlds. There are many legends that speak of the mystical hummingbird, which flies long distances and returns with messages of peace, joy, renewal, and life. Other legends tell about its ability to fly through narrow places, above the sky, or even to the center of the earth.

Mayan legends say that this bird is actually the sun in disguise, looking to court a beautiful woman, the moon. In fact, this tiny mysterious creature is often associated in legend with love and courtship. Hummingbirds are playful and fiercely independent, and during the mating ritual, males go to great lengths to get the attention of females. Well, the dapper Mr. Hummingbird got this city girl's attention this day.

After this encounter, I realized that the hummingbird also has a few things to teach us about leadership:

BALANCE

In its role as a mediator, and by the grace of its unique flight, which enables the hummingbird to hold a position mid-air, it teaches us to strive for balance. Unlike most birds, the hummingbird keeps its wings extended and moves them rapidly in a figure-eight pattern (the symbol for infinity: ∞). By producing a balance of upward and downward movement, it can hover. Even the smallest hummingbird can flap its wings at 100 beats per minute. With such rapid movement, it's not surprising that the hummingbird has one of the highest metabolisms of any bird, requiring it to consume more than its own weight in nectar each day. Yet, the hummingbird has a relatively-long lifespan compared to similar birds.

To practice hummingbird-inspired leadership, we must remember the need for balance in our lives, as well in the lives of those we lead. As we strive to achieve more and accomplish more, we must make time to replenish our supplies of nectar, the nourishing and life-sustaining results of focusing on what matters most to each of us. Balance means knowing who you are, what your priorities are, and what you need to be happy. These things are worth hovering over for a while, expending the energy to focus on what we need to make us balanced, happy *people* – and, therefore, more productive leaders and thinkers.

The individuals on your team also need balance to be productive, efficient, and innovative. And as leader, you must set a personal example of balance by working reasonable hours, having hobbies, and demonstrating priorities in your life that are not work-related. Overly focusing on business achievements will not restore you (or those you lead) to a balance that results in happiness and productivity.

Economist Carol Graham studied the effect of a financial upturn on Peruvians. Their economy had gotten so bad by 1990 that nearly 54 percent of the population was impoverished. Four years later, Peru became one of the world's fastest-growing economies. But when Graham interviewed individuals who'd experienced the most upward mobility about their newly-acquired wealth, they characterized their situations as either "negative" or "very negative." Money and achievements cannot buy happiness and may, in fact, significantly contribute to dissatisfaction. With the increased focus on wealth, their lives had fallen out of balance, and they'd lost the hummingbird's grace and self-sufficiency. The loss of balance, for hummingbirds, rich Peruvians, and leaders, means the peril of an impending crash.

SYMBIOSIS

Attracted to the beauty and fragrance of a flower, the hummingbird uses its long bill to penetrate the plant's hidden layers and lap up the elusive nectar. As the flowers support the hummingbird with their delightful juices, the bird does its part in the pollination cycle, enabling plants to mature and produce fruit and viable seeds. The grateful flowers cheer as the hummingbird moves from one to another, sustaining each of them as it is sustained by them. In fact, the bird lives on the edge, always within one day of starvation. The hummingbird and its favorite flowers have been known to co-evolve, with the shape of the bird's bill and the shape of the plants conforming over time to better fit one another.

Invoke Your Muse
Who are the flying rainbows in your life? They flit in and out of your life at just the right moment of need. They cheer for you and encourage you. They remind you to have balance in your life. They remind you of your purpose. Acknowledge them sincerely.

Likewise, hummingbird-inspired leaders and their followers co-evolve to fit one another and form strong, symbiotic unions. Under the hummingbird's leadership, everyone is fed; everyone's labors produce good fruit, within which grow the seeds of future flourishing.

At an awards program hosted by a prominent government agency, I felt the hummingbird's wisdom at work. Exceptional leaders were being recognized, leaders who, while providing day-to-day direction to staff, also created positive and productive work environments. Leaders who are like the tireless hummingbird sustain a cycle of flourishing and fruitfulness within their teams. One award recipient stood out as someone thoroughly blessed by the hummingbird. When his name was called, six people (obviously from his team) let out a tremendous cheer that pierced my heart and touched my soul. Six enthusiastic individuals had come together (early, in fact) to get adjacent seats in the crowded auditorium so they could cheer for their boss. The frantic clicks of their cameras matched the tempo of what must have been the pounding of their hearts. That man must be one heck of a leader. His flowers were cheering for him.

And *he* was cheering for *them*. True to the mutually-beneficial pollination cycle of good leadership, he flashed his team a smile as he walked down the aisle, proudly carrying his plaque. And I could tell from his face that he was proud of them. Though he was the one who walked across the stage, he knew that his team made it happen for him; his laurels rested on the fruits of their labor.

People will forgive an imperfect leader, but not a selfish one. If the hummingbird simply sucked nectar from flowers without giving back to them in the pollination process, the flowers would die – and, without its source of nourishment, so would the hummingbird. Hummingbird-inspired leaders are not self-seeking; they give back in gratitude for what they receive.

MEDIATION

Several legends describe the hummingbird's ability to move between two worlds. The Native-American Cochiti tribe tells the tale of a time when their ancestors suffered tremendous hardship due to a prolonged drought.

During this time, they lost faith in the Great Mother to bring back the clouds and restore health to their lands. Many died – people and animals. However, the hummingbird thrived. The legend credits this to the hummingbird's continued belief in the Great Mother, who rewarded the creature's faith by permitting it to pass into another world to obtain nectar and water. And a Mojave legend tells how the bird traveled a narrow, twisted path from the dark underworld to lead people to the upper world of light.

The ability to move freely between two or more worlds is an essential leadership attribute, because leadership requires understanding different groups of people, with different needs, motivations, objectives, and even languages. For example, successfully meeting sales objectives depends on an executive's ability to understand her product and the consumer world. And getting buy-in from C-level executives on a new project means stepping into the world of money to convince the CFO that it's a sound financial investment, stepping into the "big picture" world to convince the CEO that your idea will contribute to the company's long-term success, and stepping into the world where the rubber hits the road to convince the COO that your plan for making it happen will work. And successfully motivating a team requires a leader to understand and connect to people in *their* worlds in order to inspire them to greatness.

Most leadership roles require interaction at some or all of these levels. And for the hummingbird-inspired leader, who can easily and comfortably move from one world to another, and even mediate between them when necessary, hovering over the right goal at the perfect time, infinity is possible.

BENJAMIN FRANKLIN'S HUMMINGBIRD LEADERSHIP

Benjamin Franklin was an accomplished man and an extraordinary leader, one who clearly heard the hummingbird's song. A businessman, scientist, politician, diplomat, and Founding Father, Franklin authored scores of books, and his brilliance and wisdom improved the lives of all he touched. Though his innovative mind could have made him rich beyond belief, Franklin didn't aspire to be wealthy; he simply wanted to advance the efforts of all humankind. At age 42, he sold his successful printing business to pursue a career in science, believing that he could contribute more to society by producing practical discoveries that would enhance people's lives.

Jack Uldrich, author of *Leader to Leader*, writes that Franklin believed it was "shortsighted to view business activities as something separate and distinct from the community in which those businesses and their employees work and live." When this type of hummingbird-inspired thinking helped him become president of Pennsylvania, he gave his salary back to those who elected him so that it could be invested in educational projects. Today, the outcomes of his efforts are on display in science museums, including the Franklin Institute (a technology training school) and the Benjamin Franklin Institute of Technology. Incidentally, the word "museum" is derived from the word "muse," and it is obvious that Franklin listened to and was rewarded by multiple Muses.

Later, Franklin accepted the call to be ambassador to France. His collaborative style made him successful at building trust, and his ability to create win/win situations helped him find mutually-beneficial outcomes for both parties during negotiations. He once proclaimed, "We must indeed all hang together, or most assuredly we shall all hang separately." This was a man with a hummingbird-like understanding of symbiosis, earning him a reputation as one of the greatest leaders and diplomats of all time.

Chapter 22

LEADERSHIP OF THE EAGLE

"... but they who wait for the LORD shall renew their strength;
they shall mount up with wings like eagles; they shall run
and not be weary; they shall walk and not faint."

ISAIAH 40:31 (THE HOLY BIBLE, ENGLISH STANDARD VERSION)

When my brother, David, was a young boy, he decided he wanted to be a Cub Scout. We didn't have much money back in those days, so he had to wear a hand-me-down uniform. He was such a cute little Cub Scout, so handsome in navy blue. The adorable cherub needed 10 cents each week for his dues, so I hired him to teach me to play the trumpet. I was happy, because now this piano player could finally join the junior-high-school marching band, and he was happy, because the 10 cents I paid him for lessons was his ticket to one day becoming an Eagle Scout.

The rank of Eagle is awarded to scouts who demonstrate commitment, service, and leadership. Though, at that time, my encounters with eagles had been mainly through pictures, I could see the spirit of the majestic bird of prey in my little brother. I recall once, when I was in sixth grade and he was in third, a younger, smaller boy was pestering me. I was sensitive to the fact that I was much bigger than him, and the little ankle-biter was taking advantage of that. Out of the corner of my eye, I could see David running at full speed from nearly two blocks away. He was laser-focused, not unlike the eagle that swoops down, seeing nothing but his prey. Although my brother was smaller than the boy, he was not deterred. He increased momentum and didn't slow down until he knocked the jerk to the ground.

As an adult and professional bass-guitar player, David exhibits this same knock-down focus when he practices for hours on end, honing his craft. Committed to perfection, he proudly sports the merit badge of calloused fingers.

The eagle has long been considered a symbol of courage, strength, and justice. Zeus, king of the gods in Greek mythology, was always associated with the eagle, which appeared as a harbinger of victory before the successful battle with the Titans, in which Zeus vanquished his father, Kronos, and took the throne on Mt. Olympus. The grateful god-king appointed the eagle king of the birds and made him capable of soaring straight into the sun and wielding Zeus' powerful thunderbolts. The eagle was also carried into battle on a spear by the ancient Persians. Soon thereafter, the Romans adopted the tradition, and the bird came to represent the highest symbol of dignity, honor, and power.

The eagle's brave patience and unwavering strength is often invoked in *The Holy Bible.* Isaiah 40:30-31 says:

Even youths grow tired and weary, and young men stumble and fall; but those who hope in the LORD will renew their strength. They will soar on wings like eagles; they will run and not grow weary, they will walk and not be faint.

Many nations, including the United States of America, adopted the eagle as their national symbol. The eagle's virtues are universal tenets of leadership, stressing the need to overcome fear with courage, to have the stamina and resilience to press forward through adversity, and to maintain principles of truth and integrity as we continue to grow.

Eagles also teach us leadership lessons about focus, vision, hindsight, and foresight:

FOCUS

Eagles are strong, graceful, and powerful creatures. They have very muscular legs, strong talons, and powerful jaws that help them grasp and tear the flesh from prey. Eagles can lift a significant amount compared to their own body weight, and their distinctive, broad wingspan allows them to soar elegantly to great heights, to fly great distances, and to zero in on targets with laser-like precision and accuracy. But all this ferocity and power would be worthless, and the eagle would starve, if not for a keen sense of focus – just as the leader, with all her strength and power would accomplish nothing without focus and an understanding of the goals at hand.

In *The 7 Habits of Highly Effective People*, Stephen Covey writes that one must begin "with the end in mind to start with a clear understanding of your destination." This distinguishes managers concerned with just getting off the ground from leaders concerned with arriving at the right target. Effective leaders can't get distracted by minutiae. Otherwise, leading becomes a meaningless activity – more like a wild goose chase than the successful hunt the eagle must undertake to find nourishment for its young.

VISION

Eagles have keen senses of sight and hearing to aid in hunting. They have "binocular vision" like humans but can see much greater distances. At the top of the food chain, eagles are considered the most efficient, effective birds of prey. Likewise, eagle-inspired leaders see the things that others don't see – whether that's potential problems, areas for growth, changes in consumer demands, or solutions that could revolutionize the way their companies work. They paint pictures of possibilities that aren't readily apparent to others. And that vision inspires passion, purpose, and action – and inspires others to help turn things hoped for into things that can be touched, heard, and seen.

HINDSIGHT AND FORESIGHT

The Native-American Cree believed that all eagles had mystical powers, powers that could be transferred to anyone who possessed the spirit of the eagle or any part of the bird. Not only can the eagle see well in the normal sense, but its magical abilities also allow it to see far into the future and into the past. In some northern-European and Asian folk lore, the spirit of the eagle was said to enter the body of shamans and show them visions crucial to the survival of their people.

Eagle-inspired leaders learn from their past mistakes and successes, and also from those of others. Informed and intuitive, they often *anticipate* events before they unfold, making them more prepared than leaders who only focus on the here and now.

BESSIE COLEMAN'S EAGLE LEADERSHIP

Another visionary who could be classified as a human Muse, Bessie Coleman knows a thing or two about eagle-inspired leadership. The first African-American, female pilot, she soared to great heights, becoming and the first African-American to hold an international pilot's license. Like the mighty eagle, king of all the birds, she set a course for others to follow.

Born in Atlanta, Texas, the 10th of 13 children, Coleman's early educational opportunities were meager. But she loved school, especially mathematics, and excelled as a student. So she saved her money and, at age 18, enrolled in what was then the Oklahoma Colored Agricultural and Normal University in Langston, Oklahoma. But she only had enough money for one term. After that, she dropped out and moved to Chicago with her brothers.

In Chicago, she worked as a manicurist in a barbershop, where she heard fascinating tales from the pilots returning home from World War I. Coleman soon had dreams of becoming a pilot. While pursuing her lofty goal, she met an influential newspaper publisher and real-estate promoter who gave her financial backing, which helped her cause while providing the newspaper with great stories. But even with the money, she could not find an American school willing to accept and train her. She couldn't even find a black aviator willing to teach her how to fly. So she learned French and moved to Paris. There, she learned the craft quite well and excelled as a stunt pilot. Years later, she returned to the United States and became a media sensation – admired by both blacks and whites.

Bessie Coleman died at age 34 in an unfortunate aviation accident while preparing for a stunt. Coleman, who was flying with her mechanic and publicity agent, did not wear her seatbelt because she was planning to climb out onto her brand new plane. A misplaced wrench caused the control mechanisms of the plane to fail, and the subsequent spin threw her out of the plane. Perishing young and tragically, she earned her heavenly wings as a tenth Muse for generations of aspiring pilots.

Although she died before her time, Coleman's eagle-inspired leadership laid out a flight plan for many to follow. Former NASA astronaut Mae Jemison wrote in the "afterword" of Doris Rich's book, *Queen Bess: Daredevil Aviator*:

I point to Bessie Coleman and say without hesitation that here is a woman, a being, who exemplifies and serves as a model to all humanity: the very definition of strength, dignity, courage, integrity, and beauty. It looks like a good day for flying.

Coleman's dignity, strength, and courage continue to inspire generations of aviators. With focus and foresight, she soared above barriers, accessed new worlds, and opened doors that were once closed to her. Her beauty and grace captivated the masses, and she touched the lives of many. She had the eagle's vision of a different tomorrow and found her way to the future she envisioned – one where she and all like her would be able to fly.

One final point about eagles should be made. The female eagle typically lays two eggs. But the dominant chick, usually female, often kills her weaker little brother. I'm glad I didn't smother my little brother in his crib. Unlike the eagle mother, *my* mother would have stopped me … I guess. So angelic in his navy blue, David never did get his Eagle Scout wings. But today, at almost 50 years old, he still embodies eagle-leadership as a music teacher, inspiring young eaglets to soar.

Chapter 23

*"The real voyage of discovery consists not in seeking
new landscapes but in having new eyes."*

MARCEL PROUST, FRENCH NOVELIST

I recently began another all-too-frequent, recurring bout of insomnia as autumn nights approached – that time of year when air conditioning is turned off and windows are left open. The smell of the fresh fall air filled the room with a wonderful fragrance. It smelled like September.

But each night, as I lay in bed, a strange animal sound kept grabbing my attention. It was definitely a baritone voice – not the bass of a frog or the tenor of a cricket. It was rhythmical, with a pattern and frequency that clearly spoke a language I couldn't translate. The timbre was rich and thick, like molasses but not sweet – maybe like motor oil with a high viscosity but more knowing and less utilitarian. It was loud; this was no shy animal for sure. The sound was strong and confident, without the timidity you'd expect from a night-dweller.

After about a week, I finally caught sight of the culprit – a strange bird with an impressive wingspan. I first thought it was an eagle, but the head was shaped sort of funny. It was an owl.

The owl is a symbol of the feminine, the moon, and the night. It is believed to have great healing powers and is the bird of magic and darkness, of prophesy and wisdom. In Greek mythology, the owl is the sacred bird of bright-eyed Athena, goddess of wisdom, war, civilization, strength, strategy, crafts, justice, heroic endeavors, and skill. Though she is the goddess of war, Athena is known more for her cunning and craft as it applies to the strategy of battle. And the owl, with its keen vision, is often pictured perched on top of her head. In this context, the bird has gained an association with keenness, shrewdness, and knowledge acquired by study and research.

Owl-inspired leaders understand the value of vision, insight, and wisdom:

VISION

Like eagles, owls have an important message about the role of vision in leadership, or more specifically, about the necessary ability to communicate the vision with passion and purpose to your team.

In organizations, leaders see and provide the vision that inspires people to make the impossible possible and drives them to work together to accomplish what no individual could do alone. That vision becomes real and substantive through faith, good strategy, and cunning resilience. Michael Useem, in *The Leadership Moment*, discusses the overwhelming significance of vision (and action) as "the single most important lesson from [leadership] moments." He goes on to write, "Without a clear sense of destination, we are apt to flounder about, and without knowing how to get to that destination, we will never reach it even when we see it." He tells the story of Joshua Chamberlin's successful defense of Little Round Top with soldiers who, after their ammunition was depleted, charged downhill using bayonets at the Battle of Gettysburg, and compares his leadership to Lou Gerstner's successful turnaround of the all-but-dead computing giant, IBM. Both men had a vision of what the future would look like. Chamberlin saw the importance of prevailing at the Battle of Gettysburg, and Gerstner saw a future IBM, restored to its greatness and relevance. They needed their troops to buy into their visions; they needed commitment and an understanding that their paths were the right ones. And that required helping their followers to have hope, even believe, that this could be done and that any sacrifices would be worth it.

INSIGHT

Insight is defined as "an instance of apprehending the true nature of a thing," especially through intuitive understanding. Of course, insight doesn't just come from your Muse or your "gut"; it also comes from experience, knowledge, and preparedness. In *The 21 Indispensible Qualities of a Leader*, author John C. Maxwell describes how the quality of discernment applies to problem solving. Leaders are problem solvers by choice, talent, and temperament. They don't know all of the answers, but they know how to ask the right questions, seek the answers they need, and stay focused long enough to obtain the desired results. This preparedness makes them as insightful as owls, in that they are able to anticipate possible pitfalls, sense group dynamics, and make decisions based on the information they have at hand, trusting their intuitions to fill in the gaps.

Without insight, vision can be dangerous. In *The Leadership Moment*, Useem shares the tragic story of Arlene Blum, who led the first American women's team to climb Annapurna, one of the highest peaks in the Himalayas. This mountain was known for its violent winds and massive avalanches, but Blum was determined to place members of her all-female climbing team on the summit. This required bringing together 10 team members and 235 porters and Sherpas, who carried six tons of equipment on a terrain where one misstep could result in death.

While Blum had the vision for making this historic climb, she failed to consider the cost. In fact, in her enthusiasm, she failed to consider a lot of things – which taught her a brutal lesson about the challenges of leadership. The collaborative, consultative framework she established for the team worked well at 14,000 feet, but at 21,000 feet, it had fatal consequences. She failed to discern the value of insight shared by Margi Rusmore. While Rusmore was the youngest member of the team, she had made significant accomplishments in mountain climbing in high school. At age 20, she was already a highly-skilled, experienced, and intuitive climber. Though she was young, she could have been a valuable addition to the team.

Blum was not able to make the final stretch of the climb, so she permitted the two-woman team of Alison Chadwick and Vera Watson to go alone, without Rusmore. Chadwick and Watson, in their zeal to establish their place in history, convinced her that a two-person team could make it. With Blum's communal style of decision-making, she failed to discern the individual motives of those whose opinions she solicited – team members who were more focused on their own goals than the success (and survival) of the group. Blum wanted to prove to the world that women could reach great heights; Watson simply wanted to summit the Himalayas; and Chadwick wanted to summit without the need for men or oxygen. But in the end, both members of this weakened team lost their lives.

Invoke Your Muse

If you had to pick an animal as your companion
and/or messenger, what would it be? Why? You do not
need to limit yourself to one animal. Explore the
concept of your animal totem(s) in a journal entry.

WISDOM

Wisdom is defined as "a deep understanding" that helps people see the big picture and make good decisions that yield good results at little cost. A wise person has self-knowledge, is sincere and direct with others, is often asked for advice, and takes actions that are consistent with her ethical beliefs.

Wisdom should not be mistaken for education. It's the aggregation of seemingly-inconsequential bits of incomplete knowledge that the wise man transforms into a deeper understanding. In his book, *Mastering the Seven Decisions That Determine Personal Success*, Andy Andrews writes that wisdom is "an intuitive element, an insight gained from personal experience that serves us as we make choices in our lives."

True wisdom is indeed a tricky thing. History tells of many wise leaders: two Egyptian rulers, Alexander the Great and King Solomon, come to mind. They were self-aware, understood people, and found solutions to problems that didn't readily appear solvable. Humble Socrates set out to disprove the Oracle of Delphi when she called him the wisest of men. In the end, however, he realized that there was no man wiser than him, because everyone else pretended to be wiser than they were. Only Socrates was willing to admit that he knew nothing.

The wisdom of owl-inspired leaders comes to one who has readied herself by taking risks, being open to learning, and having the humility to understand and admit that she doesn't know everything.

CLIFTON WHARTON'S OWL LEADERSHIP

Clifton Wharton tapped into the spirit of the owl when he turned around the giant pension and financial-services company, Teachers Insurance and Annuity Association – College Retirement Equities Fund (TIAA-CREF). TIAA-CREF is one of the world's largest pension funds and is the retirement plan for nearly a billion college and university professors nationwide.

Wharton had a vision for a different TIAA-CREF. According to Useem, Wharton saw the organization as being so "arrogant, paternalistic, defensive, isolated, out of step, resistant to change, bureaucratic, [and] without vision, [that it] lost sight of its original purpose, lacked innovativeness, had poor communications on what it does, and poor service."

And he wanted to change all that. However, he knew better than to disenfranchise the people he would need to buy into his new vision. So he researched first, listened second, and then communicated his ideas.

Wharton's wisdom, like Socrates', was founded in his willingness to admit ignorance. Part of the magic of the owl is its ability to extract secrets. Wharton gathered critical information needed to get buy-in on his reforms – and to implement them. He traveled extensively, visiting college presidents across the country and garnering their insights and wisdom.

Believing that much-needed information could be found in non-traditional places, Wharton considered it a mistake to assume that "all information is concentrated at the apex." He felt that relying on information from the "brain trust" or the upper echelon of an organization was very limiting. To solve the great problems that challenged TIAA-CREF, he would have to get the down-low on all the areas in his organization. He was accomplished, successful, and surrounded by a diverse group of highly-educated people. So he asked for their insight, listened to their ideas, and got their feedback on his. He knew that true wisdom lives at all levels of organizational hierarchy and had the ability to focus on this.

Wharton also had the insight to discern whether his actions were effective or even appropriate. When leading academic professionals, there is usually constant debate on the relative effectiveness of any plan. But Wharton had the insight to filter through rhetoric and stay optimistic and focused on his goals. In the darkness of others' doubt, he could see the brightness of his path to success – like the owl (and the Leadership Muse), who sees best in the dark of night.

Chapter 24

LEADERSHIP LESSONS IN THE DESERT

"All the leaves are brown and the sky is gray.
I've been for a walk on a winter's day.
I'd be safe and warm if I was in L.A.
California Dreamin' on such a winter's day"

LYRICS FROM **"CALIFORNIA DREAMIN'"** BY JOHN AND MICHELLE PHILLIPS

The Leadership Muse has often delivered messages to me in the form of winged flight and strange, brave creatures. I have also found her living in what at first appears to be inhospitable and seemingly-forsaken corners of the world. I, like many leaders before me, met up with her one night in the desert.

During my first week on the job as an IT leader of a federal agency with nearly 20,000 civil servants and intense technological demands, I was sent on a whirlwind tour of the organization's three field sites in California – one near the innovation and hope of Silicon Valley, one in beautiful Southern California, nestled just below the smog, and the third in the bleak desert near the San Andreas fault. During all this travel, I de-stressed by looking out the car window. The week before, I was in my safe, warm office, working on known problems with clear resolutions at a nice desk. Now I was in a desert, listening to my two deputies discuss the previous night's meal and subsequent flatulence.

The terrain of the California desert was infinitely more interesting than their locker-room conversation. Sitting in the back seat, in artificial solitude, I was grateful for the distracting scenery – the sight of snow-capped mountains in the distance, juxtaposed with the dry, hot weather around us. But the arid bleakness of the desert could not discourage the life that broke through, peppering the sand with freckles of green. As I watched for these patches of growth in the seemingly-barren desert, the Leadership Muse whispered to me about hardship and the growth that comes during trying times.

Invoke Your Muse
What or who are the giants in your life? What are the grand challenges you are afraid to face or conquer? What have these ogres stopped you from doing?

Consider the plight of Caleb, one of two Israelites allowed into the Promised Land after 40 years of wandering the desert. In the biblical story, Moses was called to free the Hebrews from slavery under the Egyptian Pharaoh and lead them to a land promised by God. Moses sent 12 men out to scout the land. The faithful and fearless Caleb and Joshua were the only ones to bring back optimistic reports. The other 10 men returned from the mission insistent that the quest was impossible; the land was full of giants. Caleb returned proclaiming hope, saying that sure, the land was full of giants, but they were no match for the God of the Israelites, who had seen them this far. But everyone gave up – everyone except Caleb and Joshua. For their disobedience and lack of faith, God caused the Hebrews, including Joshua and Caleb by association, to wander the Egyptian deserts for four long decades.

Eventually, Joshua and Caleb were the only surviving adults from that generation of wanderers to see the Promised Land.

Caleb suffered the same punishment as everyone else – 40 years of hard labor in the desert. But during this time, his faith did not suffer and die; rather, it was sharpened and hardened into a thing of true power, earning him a place among inspired leaders. Theologian Rowland Croucher explains, "All the great leaders in the Bible had their leadership skills honed in deserts (or in prisons). Neither Caleb nor we are exempt from that rule." Indeed, Caleb's faith, wisdom, and determination in dire circumstances are qualities necessary for any leader to succeed – both in times of crisis (which *will* come) and in times of plenty.

What did Caleb learn about leadership from the Muse of the Desert, from the sandy, inhospitable place of bright stars and rare beauty? Deserts are hot, dry, barren places. There's the occasional sand dune or patch of greenery that appears on the landscape, but overall, we see very little evidence of life and few of the things needed to sustain what little life there is. Yet, in deserts as in leadership, the naked eye can't always see the miracles and lessons just below the surface. But if we focus on the distant horizon, we will find an oasis of leadership lessons to inspire and strengthen us. Desolation teaches us the meaning and purpose of our connections, and the absence of the things we think we need to sustain us teaches us resilience during the toughest of times. "Every leader," continues Croucher, writing of Caleb's eventual triumph as a leader among his people, "has to find a desert somewhere for retreat and reflection and renewal." Indeed, the nothingness of a desert is merely a mirage.

Chapter 25

"After the death of Moses the servant of the LORD,
the LORD said to Joshua ... Have I not commanded you?
Be strong and courageous. Do not be frightened, and do not be
dismayed, for the LORD your God is with you wherever you go."

THE HOLY BIBLE (ENGLISH STANDARD VERSION) JOSHUA 1:1-2, 9

Growing up in Washington, D.C., I didn't see too many Joshua trees. So during my trip across the desert, I found myself curious about the striking image of these tough trees with their relatively-slender trunks flowering into branches that stretch up to the heavens. The tufts of smiling foliage against the dark, brown branches looked to me like beautiful verdant stars in a brown heaven, symbolizing hope and promising abundant life. And when I looked on them, I heard the Leadership Muse begin to whisper about a powerful story of leadership during times of transition.

Mormon settlers named the tree as they crossed the desert to their promised land more than 2,500 years after Caleb and Joshua sought out theirs. For early settlers in the American desert, so much like the Hebrew wanderers of old, the Joshua tree was a valuable resource used for building fences and for fuel. The resourcefulness of the settlers and the ready availability of the tree are both qualities to which leaders should aspire. The shape of the tree's branches also reminded the settlers of the Bible story where Joshua's success in battle depended on arms raised up to heaven in prayer. Makes sense to me. And like the man for which it was named, the Joshua tree's deep root system makes it strong and resilient – qualities that allowed the man to survive adversity, recover from setbacks, and withstand attack. For modern day wanderers in the desert, the important thing to remember (so I've been told) is that if you lose your way so terribly that your car gets into a disagreement with a Joshua tree, the tree will win.

After several miracles, and many impossible victories in battle, Joshua became the leader who finally delivered his people into the Promised Land, illustrating the connection between faith and leadership during a time of transition. Joshua was the model of a servant-leader, supporting Moses during the Hebrews' difficult 40-year period of stress. Joshua was a strong leader in his own right, but he was closely connected with Moses, whom he believed to be called by God to lead, and Joshua knew how to follow. As a team, they were victorious in several battles. During one battle, while Moses held his arms up to heaven, Joshua was winning; when Moses dropped his arms, Joshua began to lose. Moses needed Joshua, and Joshua needed Moses.

Joshua also provides leadership lessons to those assuming new leadership roles. Moses was a tough act to follow, but Joshua's faith, resilience, and resourcefulness helped him move into his new role. Moses prepared Joshua for leadership and prepared the people for the transition. When Joshua took over, he kept his eye on the vision he shared with Moses and didn't waver. He developed plans to implement God's promise and inspired his followers with his bravery.

Both Joshua and Caleb, who never succumbed to peer pressure, gained immediate credibility after the people realized the truth and were horrified to learn that their lack of faith caused them to wander for another generation. After Moses died, Joshua never let his faith falter. He helped move the people beyond the loss of their beloved leader and into the next phase of the covenant – the Promised Land.

More than any other ancient leader, Joshua shows us how to lead through times of change. He inspired faith in others by his own example. By safely crossing the river Jordan, he proved to his people that God would hold true to his word and allow them across without casualties. During the defeat of Jericho, he inspired his followers by communicating to them a clear plan. He prepared by sending scouts out for additional information about the city's impenetrable wall, defense, weaponry, and supplies. And finally, he executed the plan with passion. His people marched around the walls rhythmically while blowing their trumpets. They did this for seven days, celebrating the end of this act of obedience and faith with shouting. Their rejoicing finally caused the walls of Jericho to come tumbling down.

Invoke Your Muse

Dedicate at least four hours each month to your own retreat, renewal, and reflection. Perhaps you are busy, but this investment of time will pay off in terms of building your leadership strength and stamina.

On the long road to Palmdale, I thought about Joshua. As we approached our destination, I snapped out of my desert daydream. Forty minutes in the desert hadn't been so bad. It had given me a chance to get to know the Joshua tree and the desert a little better. I was at a crossroad in my own career, starting out in a new leadership role, thinking about what I had learned in the past and my vision for the future. And my 40 minutes in the desert provided me with such clarity. I can only imagine what a person could learn about leadership over 40 years. I was grateful for my lesson. If the Joshua tree could thrive and survive, so could I.

When I got back from California and landed in chilly D.C., I kept humming the song, "California Dreamin." I always liked that song but never really understood the lyrics before. It's really about transition and the inevitability of leaving your warm place and moving forward into the cold discomfort of future challenges. The lyrics lament being cold "on a winter's day" and express the desire to be "safe and warm" again. I embraced my cold discomfort on this hot, summer day in a California desert, and doing so made me more receptive to the warmth of the learning that I knew would come.

Chapter 26

*"What man actually needs is not a tensionless state but
rather the striving and struggling for some goal worthy of him.
What he needs is not the discharge of tension at any cost,
but the call of a potential meaning waiting to be fulfilled by him."*

VICKTOR FRANKL, AUTHOR OF MAN'S SEARCH FOR MEANING

We are probably all familiar with the poet Robert Frost's proverb, "Two roads diverged in a wood and I – I took the one less traveled by, and that has made all the difference." I love how comedian Jerry Seinfeld counters this with his witticism: "Sometimes the road less traveled is less traveled for a reason." Whether it's the inspired action of Frost or the retrospective rationalization of Seinfeld, successful leadership moves forward, clearing a path for creativity, innovation, and calculated risk taking. And yes, sometimes this road is less traveled for a reason.

One of the worst jobs I ever had was more than a decade ago. It my first executive position in the federal government, and I knew the job would be daunting. There was an extremely difficult technology infrastructure plan that needed to be executed; I was an African-American woman in a culture that would not welcome me with open arms; and the political environment in this new agency was caustic and unforgiving. I remember that whenever I introduced myself to people and told them where I worked, I got looks of sympathy and heard the phrase, "You poor dear. Let me know if you need help." It was a job that few people wanted, and I knew that it would be difficult. But I figured someone would show me the ropes and landmines. And I believed that I had enough experience with cultural biases to work through most challenges. Soon enough, however, I saw *why* this road was less traveled.

My boss resigned one month before I started, and I had to read about it in a newspaper. My second in command, who was engaged to marry the person in charge of administrative operations, rushed through all the hiring decisions before I even started. And finally, I got a severe, 20-percent budget cut to reconcile before I ever got briefed on the budget. Each day got worse and worse.

Invoke Your Muse
We can look into our past and find times of difficulties that ended up being gifts. It was hard to see the value of those desert experiences while we were in that dry place. What are your desert experiences? How did they turn out to be life-changing moments for you?

The presidential elections in 2000 were controversial due to allegations of voting irregularities in Florida, leaving a cloud of uncertainty in the political ranks of the agency for a protracted period of time. Eventually, I was put in charge of my department (temporarily) and told to accomplish impossible tasks as assigned until a "real" CIO was appointed. I cried almost every day of this job from hell.

Finally, a colleague – a man who ended up becoming a good friend – came into my office and slammed the door behind him. He told me I needed to stop crying and do my job. He pointed out that I was strong enough technically and understood how to work in an unwelcoming culture, and he assured me I was brave enough to do what needed to be done. I needed to dry my tears and keep working through my plan.

Each day continued to get worse and worse. But I stopped crying. I made sure that my plans could be implemented without me and then resigned.

This horrible road less traveled, this job from hell, in the desert of an organization that barely gave me enough sustenance to survive, was the best learning experience of my life. I learned to be resilient. I learned to discern the truth where trust was as scarce as water in a desert and to make decisions with data given to me by lying, deceitful people. I learned to trust that the tears, the suffering, the weight gain, and the stress would be worth the learning experience if only I could hold on a few months longer. I honed the faith and determination of Moses, Joseph, and Caleb as I suffered through my own experience in an inhospitable, uncaring, and caustic wilderness.

Rowland Croucher asserts that the struggles biblical leaders encountered in the desert, even 40 years of deprivation and stalled hope, were critical in the development of their character, their faith, and their resilience. The Hebrew wanderers took many paths that were less traveled for a reason. They relied on their heroes – Moses and Aaron – to discern, through faith and determination, which roads to take and which to avoid. And then there was Joshua and Caleb, who pointed to the less-traveled path and swore it would make all the difference, which it did. But it took folks 40 years of struggling, suffering, and wanting to fully understand this truth.

Vicktor Frankl, a holocaust survivor, speaks to the tension we need to become who we are meant to be. Fear keeps us at a crossroad, but courage gives us faith and perhaps a touch of the divine madness needed to believe that the path before us will lead to a certain destiny. Suffering, when we can overcome it, gives us purpose and meaning. When we don't have the benefit of experience, or access to the experiences of others, we must rely on intuition, faith, and the subtle encouragement of the Leadership Muse to order our steps and inspire us to work until our dreams come true.

Invoke Your Muse
We have all had our desert experiences. What was yours?
Just as deserts lack water and sustenance, what did you lack?
Was it like a jungle or a rough ocean? How did you survive?

One of my favorite movie scenes is in *Indiana Jones and the Last Crusade*. Our hero, Indiana Jones, must pass three tests before he can recover the Holy Grail, one of which requires him to "step out on faith." In this test, he must cross a deep, wide cavern with no visible means of doing so. He takes a deep breath and makes the first step into thin air. Suddenly, he realizes that there is a bridge; it just matches the texture and color of the cavern so that it *appears* invisible. The test, which he passes, is to realize that it is possible to obtain his goal without any visible means to do so, to walk across a bottomless abyss to make the dream of his career come true. As he closes his eyes and takes a deep breath, he goes against everything he has learned in his academic career. Jones understands physics and gravity and the doom that lies at the base of this chasm, but he makes the first crazy step of faith that puts him on the path to his destiny. Each step is inspired by the dream of the Holy Grail as he makes his "impossible" walk to destiny. Like Caleb and Joshua, Jones hears the soft voice of the Leadership Muse in his ear, telling him that the impossible is possible.

Chapter 27

"In the desert of the heart
Let the healing fountains start,
In the prison of his days
Teach the free man how to praise."

W.H. AUDEN, BRITISH POET

Pastor and writer Rowland Croucher speaks about how the leaders who can teach us our mettle have spent time in the desert, or in prison. In the poem above, W.H. Auden casts the tone for how this happens, pairing the desert with prison as symbolic places where men heal and learn how to praise.

Martin Luther King, Jr., sharpened his focus and vision for civil rights in a lonely cell, imprisoned behind parallel bars of metal. In 1963, he penned his famous "Letter from a Birmingham Jail" as a reaction to criticism that the civil-rights battle should be fought solely in courtrooms. In his cell, he developed his message and a plan for implementing non-violent protests and civil disobedience:

Negro brothers smothering in an airtight cage of poverty in the midst of an affluent society; when you suddenly find your tongue twisted and your speech stammering as you seek to explain to your six-year-old daughter why she can't go to the public amusement park that has just been advertised on television, and see tears welling up in her eyes when she is told that Funtown is closed to

INSPIRATION FOR THE 21ST CENTURY HERO-LEADER

colored children, and see ominous clouds of inferiority beginning to form in her little mental sky, and see her beginning to distort her personality by developing an unconscious bitterness toward white people; ... when you are harried by day and haunted by night by the fact that you are a Negro, living constantly at tiptoe stance, never quite knowing what to expect next, and are plagued with inner fears and outer resentments; when you go forever fighting a degenerating sense of "nobodies" then you will understand why we find it difficult to wait. There comes a time when the cup of endurance runs over, and men are no longer willing to be plunged into the abyss of despair. I hope, sirs, you can understand our legitimate and unavoidable impatience.

It was from prison – that desert of loneliness, silence, and personal suffering – that King poured from his heart a call to action that would help end the loneliness of segregation, the silence of injustice, and the suffering endured by people of color everywhere.

Viktor Frankl, in *Man's Search for Meaning*, writes that enduring and surviving suffering helps us ultimately find purpose and meaning in life. Like King in his the Birmingham cell, Frankl began conceptualizing his book amid suffering, despair, and hopelessness as a prisoner in a Nazi concentration camp. King and Frankl have a valuable lesson for all of us, whether we endeavor to lead or just survive: Survival during suffering is really only possible when one becomes dedicated to a cause greater than himself. Holocaust prisoners lost everything – their possessions, degrees, businesses, and loved ones. The only thing left for them to hold onto was the meaning and purpose they could find in their lives. The misery evident on the surface did not diminish the beauty which lied underneath.

Frankl tells of resilience and how the human psyche can rise above the desert of suffering and misery when he writes:

We can discover this meaning in life in three different ways: (1) by creating a work or doing a deed; (2) by experiencing something or encountering someone; and (3) by the attitude we take toward unavoidable suffering.

In prison, you have no control and no possessions but you retain control over how you respond to your condition. The choice to control our response in captivity provides a freedom to rise above our apparent fate and draw upon the inner strength inherent in all of us – even the most *ordinary* of us. We survive because we know *why* we want or need to continue living. As he endured years of suffering, Frankl sought to help others find meaning, and his work has inspired generations of leaders.

The Apostle Paul spent nearly six years of his ministry in a Roman prison. However, during his imprisonment, he was upbeat, optimistic, encouraging, and faithful. Despite the horrible conditions, he demonstrated to his followers that they, like him, could draw on spiritual strength to endure. He wrote powerful letters from his cell that survive in four chapters of the New Testament: Ephesians, Philippians, Colossians, and Philemon. To the Philippians, Paul acknowledged the source of his inner strength: "I can do all things through Him who strengthens me."

Invoke Your Muse

Recall a period of suffering in your life. What was your source of inner strength? What motivated you to endure? Why did you survive that difficult time?

After my experience "imprisoned" in a C-suite, in a job so stressful and tenuous that no one else wanted it, I can certainly vouch for the fact that there's something about a desert or a prison (or a really hard time) that hones your leadership skills. Perhaps it develops your faith. Perhaps it clears out all distractions until you can finally hear the still-small voice of your Muse. It may lower your inhibition to be a little crazy and simultaneously strengthen your resolve and endurance for performing the impossible tasks that leadership often requires. Or maybe it helps you answer one of life's most important questions: *Why* do you need to act, live, believe, or lead?

In hindsight, my desert experience in that horrible job helped me learn some of my most valuable lessons about leadership. I overcame difficult challenges and emerged bruised but stronger. In order to endure, survive, and succeed, I had to *dig deep* within my core in order to reach the finish line, and there I found out so much about myself and my strength.

The next time you are in a desert or prison in your own life or career, when you look around at your scarce resources, dig deep and choose instead to see life, and life abundant, because you are in the perfect place to find faith, stamina, courage, and an oasis of purpose and meaning.

chapter 28

"Heroic leaders have an unselfish devotion to the interest of others. Their mission is to energize other people, and to bring out the best in them. Further, heroic leaders view themselves as an instrument for helping others attain goals, satisfy needs, and reach their potential. They put others before them."

IRA J. MORROW, AUTHOR OF
DEFINING A NEW TYPE OF ORGANIZATIONAL LEADER: THE HEROIC LEADER

Who has seen the Desert Horseman? He's an ordinary person who is actually a hero in disguise, a common man or woman whose pleasant demeanor hides a wealth of uncommon wisdom, someone you barely notice, who rides into moments of your life then off again into the sun.

My Desert Horseman is just such a paradox – an unexpected mystery and a familiar friend. A simple man who lives a modest life in one of the poorest states in the United States, his aspiration is to make sure that his family has enough food to eat and a roof over their heads. He doesn't have a fancy education or any college degrees but is very well-read and intelligent. He can fix things too. You could call him the Desert MacGyver; skilled like the resourceful character on the 1985 television program, he could probably build a spaceship with recycled junk, duct tape, and a soldering iron. This simple man, the stranger in the desert, is an oasis of wisdom and inspiration that reflects the understanding of not one, but several lifetimes.

He's an ordinary man, above average in height and below average in weight. He's solemn, serious, stubborn, and opinionated, living a life as isolated as his habitat. He has nice hair, bad teeth, and a warm heart. He quietly observes life, characters, and events. He believes in destiny and purpose and is passionate about the things in life that matter most. His dark eyes and somber expression mask the wisdom beneath, wisdom most someone could only gain over several lifetimes.

My Desert Horseman is a real person – warm and made of flesh, with blood running through his veins. And though I've never met him in person, this desert hermit reached out to me, a D.C. diva, to teach me about hero-leadership and to provide guidance and instruction that would change my life.

Several years ago, I decided that I, being a technologist, should evaluate the use of social media as a leadership and communication tool. I began blogging and found it surprisingly effective at disseminating information to my stakeholders. But I was unprepared for how this technology would help me connect with the soul of a hero hiding in the desert. Suddenly, this extraordinary, ordinary man began sending me inspirational messages, then leadership advice, mentoring, counsel, and intuitive insight – all the things a girl needs to make it through the day.

My Desert Horseman wasn't a *Fortune* 500 executive leadership coach, but he understood people and carefully observed society around him. He encouraged me to leverage my empathetic skills and to risk reaching out and connecting to people in more authentic ways. He emphasized the virtue of truth – truth in my interactions with people, truth in my ethical foundation, and being true to myself about who I am and what I stand for. He encouraged me to dig deep, to find my passion around my goals as a leader, and to use those emotions to fuel the energy that would ignite my dreams to burn through into reality. From 3,000 miles away, the under-standing from this mysterious man helped me better utilize my talents.

I say I've never met him face to face. However, I suspect I might have seen him without knowing it. Perhaps we have all seen him – and mistaken him for someone ordinary. Like Clark Kent's spectacles and the Lone Ranger's mask, the Desert Horseman's "regular-guy" image disguises an abundance of knowledge, magic, and power. He was probably the stranger who stopped along the road to change your tire or the heroic passerby who sprang into action to save a drowning little boy, or maybe he's the unsung hero who breathed life back into a heart-attack victim. All he wants in return is truth and justice – and a can of sardines or a grilled cheese sandwich.

In his scholarly paper, "Defining a New Type of Organizational Leadership: The Heroic Leader," Ira J. Morrow lists the qualities of heroes – including determination, courage, unselfishness, risk taking, and self-sacrifice – and asserts that if we bring these heroic traits into our leadership styles, we can better meet today's organizational challenges. As organizations become more successful, they have a tendency to become more bureaucratic. Despite the negative connotation, bureaucracy is actually a positive outcome from the industrial age. With bureaucracy – or the formal systems of institutions – we can better manage risks. And believe it or not, this has its value. Bureaucracy provides consistent and impersonal ways of managing authority, responsibility, recordkeeping, and the uniform application of rules. It helps ensure that regulations are consistently applied, which is particularly important in life-saving organizations like hospitals or government agencies like the Food and Drug Administration. In organizations where there is a societal need for equal treatment, it offers free access and the elimination of favoritism or cronyism. And it provides an efficient, effective ways to organize tasks too large or complex for most people to understand.

However, when organizations become *driven* by bureaucracy, they also limit the opportunities for hero-leaders to work their magic, to apply the bravery, determination, risk-taking courage, and faith that are their tools. Hero-leaders are brave. However, it's becoming more and more difficult to find leaders willing to take on tough or controversial issues and problems. Hero-leaders are willing to break rules at the right times, to confront difficult people, and to take a stand on issues of value, ethics, or principles, even when it makes them unpopular. They aren't reckless, but like Joshua, they command enough facts or intelligence to be ready for any adverse consequences.

Invoke Your Muse

Who are your Desert Horsemen? They are the ordinary men or women in your life that almost go unnoticed – the undercover angels that bless and inspire us continuously. They could be grandmothers, bartenders, subway passengers, or even strangers.

John C. Maxwell discusses many of these heroic traits for today's leader in his book, *The 21 Indispensible Qualities of a Leader*. Like heroes old and new, good leaders must act a little crazy at times to overcome fear and do what scares them. They must occasionally take risks in order to achieve what many believe is impossible. They must put others first and not let selfish desires for things like money or possessions take their minds off servitude. And like Indiana Jones, who overcomes his fear and takes a step of blind faith, hero-leaders must actually believe in what they do – with all their hearts.

Worried that you aren't like the Desert Horseman – born heroic? In his article, "Are Heroes Born, Or Can They Be Made?" Jonah Lehrer tells us that heroes are just ordinary people who do extraordinary things – and that we can all perform heroic feats by: (1) not allowing evil to flourish, (2) becoming more empathetic and attentive to the needs of others, (3) internalizing heroic vision or imagination, and (4) putting these new behaviors into action. And Edmund Burke tells us, "All that is necessary for the triumph of evil is that good men do nothing." Thus, heroism begins by recognizing what needs to be done, believing that you can do it, and putting belief into action. In this way, we can all become heroes by taking Indiana Jones' step of faith, Moses' leap of faith, or Lehrer's four steps to faith.

As I learned more about my hero in the desert, I found out that as a grocery store worker, he saved the life of a heart-attack victim. While enjoying a pleasant day in the New Mexico sun, he saved a drowning boy. There are more stories, I know, but he is reluctant to share. Yet, he freely points out examples of hero-leadership in others and offers mentoring and guidance from thousands of miles away. He's saved señoritas in sorrow and divas in leadership distress, and afterwards, returned to his fortress of solitude for a cold can of beer and a slice of hot pizza.

The Desert Horseman, who also recognized his Muse when he met her, told me an amazing tale about a diminutive pony named Freckles. That ornery horse would bite, spit, and kick, and no one wanted to risk riding the horse that didn't want to be ridden. But the young Desert Horseman, encouraged by his grandpa, saw greatness in this miniscule stallion. Knowing that he had to hold onto the horse's mane or fall, he found the courage to command the ill-mannered animal. I don't know what that skinny, little boy saw in that bad-tempered pony, but he had a vision of a future where it was a great steed, and he refused to give up and walk away.

My friend didn't have the privilege of riding the most desirable horses, so he took the road not traveled – the horse no one wanted to ride. His intuition provided him with all the instruction he needed. And his courage gave him the confidence and strength to tame the untamable.

So the boy conquered and transformed Freckles into a small but mighty stallion – and transformed himself into a man.

I don't know why the story of a skinny, little hero who loved an unlovable horse moved me. But woven into this story, I see and understand some of the key leadership principles that Maxwell and Lehrer define, and that Joshua and Caleb exemplified – courage, belief in the impossible, selfless heroism, risk-taking, a little divine madness, and speaking truth to power, even when you are outnumbered.

Again, we've all seen the Desert Horseman. We just didn't notice him, just as we look out on the vast nothingness of a desert without seeing the miracles and lessons hidden there. If you travel west from Washington, D.C., and drive through El Paso, Texas, passing cacti, tumbleweeds, Joshua trees, and waves of brown nothingness, you'll arrive at beautiful, white sand dunes, which give the miraculous illusion of snow in the desert. Past that, in the middle of New Mexico, you'll find my Desert Horseman. His name is David. You may not notice him at first, but he'll remind you of another David – one who started off as a little boy with a rock and a slingshot and whose hero-leadership conquered a giant and transformed a group of desert wanderers into a mighty nation.

That little David, from Caleb's tribe of Judah, met a descendent of one of the giants Caleb and Joshua didn't fear. The giant, Goliath, taunted the Israelites for 40 days before David volunteered to slay the fearsome tyrant. David didn't worry about being small and outmatched against the giant, even though the king's entire army was afraid. He was too small to wear armor, so dressed in a simple shepherd's tunic, he used a sling and a well-placed stone to subdue the menacing creature.

Often, we have to conquer the giants in our own minds before we can perform the heroic acts required of us. In *Gulliver's Travels*, Jonathan Swift paints a portrait of the tiny Lilliputians, who fearlessly conquer the mighty "giant," Gulliver. And Gulliver must conquer his giant ego to convince his tiny captors – through humility and submissiveness – to release him. Gulliver explains:

My gentleness and good behavior had gained so far on the emperor and his court, and indeed upon the army and people in general, that I began to conceive hopes of getting my liberty in a short time.

We often have our own Freckles in life, impediments that we conquer with a lot of heart and a little saddle; then we grow up and save lives, work hard, and raise our kids. We also have our own Goliaths, tyrants who would stand in our way and attempt to taunt us into inaction; then we grow up and lead nations. I had my Freckles. I had my giants. And I learned what to do – thanks to a tree, a few Hebrew wanderers, and a desert hermit with a touch of divine madness.

part four
Profile of the Hero–Leader

chapter 29

"When we get scared and selfish, these brave souls find a way to act, to speak out, to help others in need. That's why they're heroes."

JONAH LEHRER, AUTHOR OF ARE HEROES BORN, OR CAN THEY BE MADE?

Just like infinity is a really big number that can get bigger and bigger, organizational and societal problems just keep getting harder and harder; the stakes keep getting higher; and the risks keep getting riskier. So the demand for hero-leaders like the Desert Horseman also grows.

I recall a colleague telling me that his job was impossible, because he needed more people, a bigger budget, and more time to get things done. Hell, with more people, more money, and more time, *anyone* could do the job, right? But these are the realities a leader must face – budgets that just keep getting tighter, human resources that have become scarcer, and pressure to get things done that doesn't quickly let up. These exceptional challenges require more than ordinary abilities. Leaders must become more heroic.

If hero-leaders can leap tall buildings in a single bound, then ordinary, or mediocre, leaders limit themselves to hopping over small structures. They simply don't take on the big challenges and are not prepared for the scale and scope of most of the problems that are presented. If hero-leaders are faster than speeding locomotives, then ordinary leaders can't keep up with the pace of change. They stumble and fall, and challenges and opportunities pass them by. Nassir Ghamei, in *A First Rate Madness*, notes that successful political or military leaders are rarely what we would consider normal or ordinary. This is because it takes a certain amount madness to inspire leaders to leap those tall buildings and move faster than speeding locomotives.

In the *Lexus and the Olive Tree*, Thomas L. Friedman talks about the "winners take all" global environment in which we operate today. He writes that the potential market for "any good or service, for any singer or songwriter, for any author or actor, for any doctor or lawyer, or any athlete or academic, now extends from one end of the world to the other." What was smaller and known becomes much larger and unknown as the business world becomes increasingly global in its scope, and ordinary leadership is not sufficient in this new economy. Risks have become more risky, so ordinary leaders are less willing to take the chances that would move them beyond infinity.

In the same sense that our markets and spheres of influence are global, our problems have become matters of international concern as well. Consider the role of businesses and human inaction in the BP oil disaster, hurricane Katrina, the Haitian earthquake, or the ordeal of the trapped Chilean and West Virginian miners. These events will continue to increase, and the bar for performance, and for finding solutions and creating alternatives, will keep getting higher and higher. Our times demand a new kind of leader, one touched by divine madness and the favors of the Muse. Our times require the hero-leader.

The Homeric Greek hero of ancient times was a man who was more than human but less than divine. The word "hero" literally means "demigod," and many Greek heroes had one parent who was a god and one who was human. Today's hero, on the other hand, is someone distinguished by exceptional courage, nobility, and fortitude – a person recognized for possessing superior, or nearly divine, qualities in her chosen field. A *leader* must influence groups of people to accomplish a certain goal, whereas the *hero*, even in the ancient stories, usually works alone. But today's *leaders* must mobilize groups of individuals to work in concert, to collaborate, and to be inspired and motivated by the same goal. Indeed, leaders in our time and place must be able to do the impossible and the improbable – and because they *can't* do it alone, they must be able to give as much inspiration as they get. Thus, the *hero-leader* is born.

In ancient myths, the Muses sat beside their father, Zeus, and sang of the wonderful acts performed by Greek heroes like Achilles, Odysseus, Jason, and Prometheus. By praising heroic feats, the Muses exercised tremendous influence and further encouraged others to perform acts of bravery and valor. The Leadership Muse bestows the same gift; she adds that little extra bit to the infinity leaders and heroes strive for. And in doing so, she makes heroes out of good leaders and leaders out of good heroes – giving rise to the hero-leaders our world so desperately needs. And like the nine original Muses, she makes those who hear her song of inspiration infinitely greater.

When we grappled with the concept of infinity, we learned that when we think there is an upper bound – where *n* represents the largest possible number, the most excellent day, the most ideal website, the tastiest roast chicken, the most beautiful poem, the best we can possibly be – we can just add a bit more (+1) and have something even bigger and better. The Muse helps add that little something more to those she inspires. When you've practiced to perfection and are able to dig even deeper to win a competition, even though you were the underdog, that's the Muse's influence. When you invent something revolutionary, even though everyone thought there was nothing new under the sun, or you save the homeless when it seemed that one person couldn't make a difference, that's the Muse's influence. Just when you think there is nothing else possible to add, nothing more you can do, nothing new to think, the Muse can add more – giving you the jumpstart needed to approach infinite and heroic capabilities.

While the Leadership Muse's blessings are worth the risk, a warning is necessary; we must remember the divine madness. She often inspires hero-leaders with so much single-minded passion that they can come across as insane or frantic to the unaware. But though the Leadership Muse may inspire actions that seem insane to the outside observer, she will bring hero-leaders to the height of brilliance, just like the Muses of old brought fame to poets everyone thought deranged. She will inspire and help mold the hero-leader by whispering in his ear, motivating and encouraging him to press forward to his greatness, even and in spite of naysayers, doubters, and ill-wishers. Maybe you doubt the existence of this fantastic spirit. To be convinced, all you need do is call upon her and watch for her to show herself. The Leadership Muse exists insofar as we recognize the feats of the hero-leader, who is the focus of her work. Accounts of the hero-leader's feats of greatness spread like wildfire, flames fanned by the Muse, and inspire others to follow in his footsteps.

Just as there is no upper limit to the challenges and problems presented by this world of ours, there is no limit to what hero-leaders can do, at least not when there is a Muse on hand to help us find that little something extra. Infinity is her horizon. Luck is taken out of the equation, because she causes things to happen, rather than relying on "random" outcomes. We've seen ordinary people face impossible situations with super-human strength and divine inspiration. Of course, hero-leaders know that this is not magic; it is simply the result of inspiration from the Leadership Muse.

chapter 30

PORTRAIT OF A HERO-LEADER

"That's what it takes to be a hero, a little gem of innocence inside you that makes you want to believe that there still exists a right and wrong that decency will somehow triumph in the end"

LISE HAND, AUTHOR

Hero-leaders have all of the characteristics of ordinary leaders, plus certain stellar qualities that make them extraordinary. Preparation, practice, and stamina are character traits that help us recognize hero-leaders. We also recognize them by their ethics, focus, and faith. They have capes, too, but wearing them is often optional.

It helps to describe the hero-leader by looking at what makes someone a bad leader. Bad leaders tend to be selfish or greedy. They want more money, success, comfort, or power. A bad church leader will make sure that he is driven around in a limousine while the mortgage on the building is in default. The ordinary or lazy leader tends to give more thought to self-preservation or protection, taking few risks and realizing little gain. You may see her leading a ministry to feed the homeless but unwilling to venture out into the neighborhoods where they seek shelter. For example, former televangelist James Bakker used his followers' money to acquire material wealth and satisfy his sexual appetites. He was convicted of fraud in 1998 after lining his own pockets with more than $3 million dollars that people donated to his ministry. Not until he sat in a prison cell, broken and alone, did he realize that his selfishness had led him way, way off track.

The ordinary or lazy leader will manifest this trait in lesser extremes and say things like: "That's beyond my pay grade," "It's too hard, "That's impossible." "It's not part of my job description," or "I'm too low on the totem pole to make a difference." But good leaders, like Mohandas Gandhi, consider the needs of others far more important than their own. Though he commanded no army, Gandhi was victorious over nations. Though he could have been rich, this humble man was self-sufficient and lived modestly. And in 1948, he paid the ultimate price for his people and his faith – his life.

While hero-leaders are forward-thinkers, bad leaders are focused on the past. Every era looks back with disdain at earlier generations. Even back in the good old days, there were people talking about the "good old days." Things were never as ideal as they used to be – even when they *were*. The challenges of the present always seem to exceed the challenges of the past. But as the world keeps getting smaller and our interconnected problems keep getting bigger, the hero-leader must intervene. The ancient Romans leaders never figured that out. Their problems seemingly got easier and easier. Yet, they were never able to conquer their biggest enemy – the success of their past generations. And in the end, their over-confidence cost them an empire.

Bad leaders maintain their power by making their followers completely dependent. On the other hand, hero-leaders know that they can accomplish more if they empower their followers to be self-reliant, even heroic in their own right. In *Company of Heroes: Unleashing the Power of Self-Leadership*, Henry Sims and Charles Manz talk about creating the Super Leader, one capable of creating followers who are self-leading heroes. They insist that such transformation will unleash the "talent, energy, enthusiasm, and expertise of everyone in the organization." And creating such an environment, such a productive ecosystem, will also increase the chances of overcoming the economic, diplomatic, and ethical challenges with which individuals and organizations are endlessly confronted.

Hero-leaders share power and information. Leaders can no longer maintain power by limiting information. The World Wide Web has leveled the playing field by providing information and knowledge to anyone with access to the Internet and a computer. Furthermore, leaders who hoard important organizational information limit themselves because they violate what John C. Maxwell calls "The Law of Exponential Growth." Their followers must rely on them for all the answers, and they end up spending most of their time fielding questions.

Invoke Your Muse
What "ordinary" traits do you have that could help make you an extraordinary leader? And just for fun, what does your cape look like?

On the other hand, hero-leaders communicate clearly with their teams, saving themselves time that would have been wasted micromanaging, and earning the trust and respect of their followers. Michael Useem, in *The Leadership Moment*, recounts the story of Joshua Chamberlain, a Union officer who led his men during the critical Battle of Gettysburg. Chamberlain was charged with a large group of soldiers, most of whom wanted to desert. So he brought them together, listened to their concerns, and then shared as much information as he could, empowering them with the choice to either stay and fight, or leave without retribution. Most stayed and helped successfully defend Little Round Top, giving the Union army a key victory and a significant tactical advantage.

Hero-leaders teach others how to also be resourceful leaders, capable of developing new followers and stronger teams. The power and influence of the 21st-century hero-leader grows not just through her followers but through her follower's followers. Useem also writes about hero-leader Nancy Barry, president and founder of Enterprise Solutions to Poverty, whose global organization raised more than $1 billion dollars of capital for women in third-world countries. Committed to eradicating poverty, Barry made it possible for women to get small "micro-loans" to start businesses and become self-sufficient. Just $30 to these struggling mothers was the difference between a new life and starvation for their families, and Barry gave them the chance to change their own lives.

Today's hero-leaders must create leaders capable of creating other leaders by sharing information, responsibility, and successes. They must be generous and think of others before they think of themselves. And they must believe, and make others believe, that the impossible is possible.

Chapter 31

"The only thing we have to fear is fear itself."

FRANKLIN D. ROOSEVELT, 32ND PRESIDENT OF THE UNITED STATES

Becoming a hero-leader requires constant work. Though I felt the pull of inspiration and heard the voice of the Leadership Muse, on many occasions, I took a moment to admire her song and did nothing with her guidance. I was a lazy leader.

In the fifth grade, I was a pretty good sprinter. I could beat most people on the team at my school in urban D.C. – except for one girl. But that really didn't matter, because I didn't have to race her; I just had to beat the slow pokes from other schools. Then one day, the coach forced me to race her. I got a great start on the 50-yard dash and beat her off the block. Though she caught up to me, I was still beating the fastest girl in northeast Washington, D.C. But just as I came within reach of the finish line, she passed me with a smile on her face. The coach told me that I did very well and that with a little work, I could be a champion sprinter. I was tired and went home. I never ran after that. This was one of the early signs of my lazy leadership. Being born a leader, like being born smart, or fast, or being able to read music, is a gift. But taking that gift and applying perspiration to the inspiration is what makes a *hero*-leader. Yes, as a sprinter, I had the gift of speed. But I lacked motivation and was too lazy to cross the finish line.

In his dialogue praising divine madness, Plato cautions against behaviors likely to repel and repulse the Muse. He writes of a conversation between Socrates and his young friend, Phaedrus, about cicadas. Socrates explains that those summertime bugs that haunt hot evenings with their dry, monotonous song, were once human artists so obsessed with their art and mad with love that they forgot to eat, drink, or sleep. Their fate? Death, of course. But their souls lived on. Moved by pity and gratitude, the Muses transformed these lovesick souls into cicadas and rewarded them with the ability to sing constantly, from birth to death, never needing to eat or sleep.

Invoke Your Muse
What's tugging at your sleeve? How are you being called out of laziness? Are you even listening? What is holding you back from action?

The cicadas, Socrates told Phaedrus, also became the Muses' spies, watching mortals to see which ones would be lulled into laziness and which ones would sustain the inspiration to sing, dance, and create good work. Laziness is the Muses' greatest enemy, as it brings certain death to inspiration. The lazy leader will squander the gifts of the Leadership Muse, like I did for many years – until the Muse finally got my attention.

I was insulted once by a boss who said I was lazy. I was working long hours and killing myself trying to keep my head above water. I endured stressful conditions and managed to deliver some much-needed capability to my organization. This didn't seem to be the work of a lazy girl. Yet, in hindsight, I realize that my boss was right. Though I was always busy and working, my laziness manifested itself in a reluctance to do the harder things – to help, learn, and grow.

After I got my first supervisory position, I excelled as a manager but resisted the move to a true leadership position. As a manager, I knew how to execute the tasks in my technical specialty effectively. I was very good at this and quite comfortable with it. However, *leadership* required not just performing tasks effectively, but also knowing what needed to be done. Peter Drucker best describes this distinction: "Management is doing things right; leadership is doing the right things." At the time, it seemed easier to sit back and offer criticism of leadership than to actually become part of the solution.

When I finally made my first move into a leadership position, my motivations were less about wanting to make a difference and more about not wanting to be told what to do. Obedience was never my strong suit (it still isn't, actually), and I wanted to be a leader because I wanted to be the boss. However, I was misguided (and lazy) in accepting this position, not having taken the time to learn that a key component of successful leadership is being able to follow and serve.

Eventually, the skill sets that made it easy for me to see problems and criticize caught up with me. I had a boss who used to move me around the organization to solve his problems. There was a look that he always gave me when he was about to reassign me. When I saw that look, I would try to steer clear of him, but at some point, he would catch up with my husband (who worked with me at the time) and pass on the message that I couldn't avoid him forever. Lazy leaders avoid problems and don't want to get their hands dirty. They sit back and criticize when they should be looking for opportunities to lend their talents to the organizations they serve.

Just as Jim Collins says, "Good is the enemy of great." Likewise, smart is the enemy of learning. When another boss decided to send me to leadership training, I was angry. How could someone as smart as me need training? I went to the so-called training and was bored because of the pace and the trite content. I complained every chance I got. Finally, I spoke to one of the facilitators, who encouraged me to stop focusing on everything I already knew and instead look for nuggets of wisdom that I didn't know. Lazy leaders don't look for opportunities to learn; they assume they already know everything and fail to see the infinite wisdom life has to offer.

Rounding out my litany of laziness is an unwillingness to grow. We all get into our comfort zones – where we feel safe, competent, and strong – but we limit ourselves as leaders when we refuse to step out of the known. One of my first forays into unsafe and uncomfortable places was at a conference on what then was an emerging technology – the World Wide Web. I had no interest in the topic, met people I didn't want to know, and being stuck in an unfamiliar, rural city, had no way to even escape for a decent meal. Looking back, it is clear that I squandered an opportunity to learn and possibly even shape technologies that were just being invented. But it was too difficult and foreign to me. Lazy leaders don't want to grow, so they overlook opportunities to expand and strengthen their talents. The status quo is good enough for them.

My Muse was getting impatient. Inspiration was always tugging at my sleeve, prompting me to help others, to learn, and to grow. But from sprinting, to studying, to missed career opportunities, my own hidden laziness delayed what should have been inevitable. Overcoming this laziness required me to first acknowledge the sources of inspiration all around me and then to understand how inspiration profoundly affected me – personally and as a leader.

chapter 32

"Fatigue makes cowards of us all."
VINCE LOMBARDI, FOOTBALL COACH

Hero–leaders are *prepared* to accomplish their impossible goals, even if doing so requires training to the point of exhaustion. Under the leadership of Vince Lombardi, the NFL-championship Green Bay Packers team spent such long and intense hours on practice and drills that some players dropped on the field from exhaustion. When Buster Douglas beat Mike Tyson against all odds, he was well-trained and in the best physical shape of his life. And Lou Gerstner, the CEO who made IBM the force it is today, speaks of the need for leaders with the requisite stamina to press forward towards impossible goals.

Lombardi is regarded as one of the best coaches in history. He became the head coach of the Green Bay Packers after they finished a season with one win and 10 losses. Believing in the importance of physical conditioning, he established a rigorous training camp. In his first season, the much-improved team finished with a seven-five record. At the end of his second year, he took the team to the championship and nearly won. And for the next two seasons, he led Green Bay all the way to the championship.

Lombardi's approach to getting impossible performance from his players is described in *Vince Lombardi's Winning Ways*: "He took the measure of each athlete to find the precise blend of confidence and fear that would call forth the best football he was capable of playing." Lombardi demanded that each player do his personal best to use his God-given talent, so they didn't stop practicing until they were exhausted and in pain. At that point, he pushed them to give a bit more. And he ensured them that every loss was a victory with learning opportunities.

Lombardi's leadership style attracts followers who give their best (plus a little bit more) and produce unlikely results and unbelievable outcomes – on the football field, at work, or in life. That kind of leadership will also convince a collective of people in a slow-moving organization to give a little bit more of themselves in order to achieve greatness they never imagined possible.

PREPARATION AND FAITH

"Watch the turtle. He only moves forward by sticking his neck out."

LOU GERSTNER

Faith prepares hero-leaders for achievement. Having faith and believing in what they are doing and why sustains them while they tirelessly push, fight, and work and gives them evidence that they will prevail and that victory is inevitable. They are not delusional; instead, they possess an honest and sincere optimism which knows that "impossible" is only a word. They are focused on outcomes and keep their eyes on the desired results, even if it means taking a calculated risk or two.

In his book, *Who Says Elephants Can't Dance*, Lou Gerstner talks about taking on the "impossible" task of saving IBM:

IBM sales and profits were declining at an alarming rate. More important, its cash position was getting scary ... I was convinced that ... the odds were not better than one in five that IBM could be saved and that I should never take the position.

But he took the position anyway – and revolutionized the company by making the customer his number one priority. The customer's desire for quality and performance drove his vision and market focus. His secrets for accomplishing this impossible feat were focus, being superb at execution, and using the full potential of personal leadership.

STAMINA AND ETHICS

"Yes, it's Superman, strange visitor from another planet, with powers and abilities far beyond those of mortal men! Superman, who can change the course of mighty rivers, bend steel with his bare hands, and who, disguised as Clark Kent, mild-mannered reporter for a great metropolitan newspaper, fights a never-ending battle for truth, justice and the American way!" – from the 1950s TV show, Superman

Invoke Your Muse

Did you ever get close to reaching a goal but didn't quite make it across the finish line? Did you run out of energy? Why? How can you modify your behavior and learn to use your skills effectively for success next time?

Hero-leaders never lose sight of the goodness of their purpose and they have the staying power that permits them to press on until they succeed. Hero-leaders are *good*. They are unselfish and driven by altruism – not for the money, not for self-aggrandizement, but for the sake of doing something good. They may do it to make a deceased mother proud, like Buster Douglas, or for the sake of meeting a grand challenge, like Lou Gerstner, or simply for the love of the sport, like Vince Lombardi. The hero Luke Skywalker in the *Star Wars* films battles against the wrongness of the "dark side," which gives him the endurance to come back and fight through his own physical and emotional pain. As a hero-leader, it's not what's in it for *him*, but what's in it for those he serves and protects.

On the other hand, Andrew Fastow was the highly-skilled chief financial officer for Enron. He certainly had leadership qualifications that landed him that top spot, but he lacked the ethics to do the job successfully. His selfish desire to acquire wealth and impress his boss by any means necessary drove him to ruin the company and the financial livelihood of many people.

If the cicadas are indeed the spies of the Muses, they are on the lookout not just for those of us who stay awake, but those who stay vigilant. It is only those whose hearts and minds are in the right place, who can keep their eyes open, and whose ears stand ready so that they might catch a hint of the inspiration offered by the divine voice of the Muse.

Chapter 33

RECOGNIZING YOUR OWN GIFTS AND SUPER POWERS

*"When we embrace what lies within, our potential
knows no limit. The future is filled with promise.
The present, rife with expectation."*

MOHINDER, FICTIONAL CHARACTER FROM THE 2006 TV SHOW **HEROES**

Heroes, a science-fiction series that ran on NBC from 2006 to 2010, quickly became one of my favorite TV shows. A group of special people discovers that they possess super-human powers and abilities. As they learn to use their powers, they struggle to cope with the impact that being special has on their lives. Some want to use the powers for selfish purposes – to make money, seek power, and even rule the world. Some want to figure out how to use their powers for good. Often, the supernaturally-inclined good guys (or heroes) must come together and use their combined powers to save the world.

I relate to these heroes. I understand them because I am one of them. So are you, though you may not know it yet. Like these characters, your powers may be slowly emerging. Hidden within you are abilities you may not even suspect – hidden stores of strength and ancient wisdom that elude the thinking, analytical mind.

You may prefer to deny your special abilities, because calling yourself a hero seems like the egotistical assertion of a narcissistic lunatic. Why would I think I am that special? Why should you? Why would I succumb to these delusions of grandeur? Why should you?

Don't listen to the naysayers. Doubt is kryptonite. I am a hero. I will not deny this anymore, nor should you, or any person who is willing to believe in the impossible and wants to achieve miracles. Today's leader *must* be heroic.

Listening to the Leadership Muse will help you cultivate your hidden, intrinsic powers. And of course, to whatever strengths and talents you think you have, the Muse will add a little bit more. She may even inspire you into a temporary state of insanity whereby you forget your limitations, overcome your fears, and press forward with passion, power, and purpose, doing the things that hero-leaders are called upon to do.

Invoke Your Muse
Who or what is your kryptonite? Think of external obstacles and internal blocks. Old habits? Negative voices in your head and in your environment?

Comparing supernatural powers to leadership skills may seem pretentious or a bit of a stretch, but doing so makes it possible for anyone to develop and grow powerful heroic-leadership abilities. And many of the most popular super powers translate well into the leadership arena. The journey of finding those hidden leadership skills begins with humble self-examination and acknowledgement of our masked potential.

Let me attempt a dispassionate description of my super powers, which I have cultivated during my continuous journey to becoming a hero-leader. They are empathy, telepathy, clairaudience, and clairvoyance.

Chapter 34

THE EMPATH:
ABLE TO LEAP INTO A PERSON'S HEART IN A SINGLE BOUND

*"Leadership is about empathy. It is about having the
ability to relate and to connect with people for the
purpose of inspiring and empowering their lives."*

OPRAH WINFREY

I didn't have the word "empathic" for this superpower until I met Marilou, a wonderful lady I was interviewing to be my executive coach. I really didn't want a coach. I didn't want anyone that deep in my head. But my leadership team needed to develop their skills, so I asked them to each to get a coach. Therefore, I had to set an example and eat my own dog food.

I skimmed all of the résumés with disinterest but was drawn to Marilou's, so I set up an appointment with her. We had a nice conversation – until she asked, "Why did you choose me?" I told her it was because she seemed like an interesting person and that I thought her background in drama would benefit me. She confirmed my thinking, but went on to discuss other relevant parts of her background. Then she stunned me by saying that her bio made no mention of drama. I insisted it was there. She denied it again. I looked for the proof in her résumé, and sure enough, it wasn't there. I was perplexed.

Thank goodness Marilou understood what was happening. When she saw my confusion, she explained that I was *empathic*. I was able to discern her love of acting from the words on a sheet of paper – which said nothing about drama – or perhaps from something I had picked up on during our meeting.

I started to cry, revealing (and releasing) the years of pain I endured from being able to sense other people's thoughts and feel their emotions. That understanding is a heavy load to bear, one I had not realized that I was carrying. The emotional reaction startled me, but Marilou remained unshaken. She gave me some tissue and told me that through specific coaching, I could learn to use this power for good – if only I would stop denying it.

As a leader, being aware of people's feelings is a huge responsibility for me – a time-consuming and complicated one. If I could hide the fact that I know what my followers think and feel, I could continue to ignore them and go along my lazy way. It would be easier. Furthermore, I am not just aware of how they feel; I actually *feel* it. I didn't realize until that encounter with Marilou that if I stopped pushing it away and allowed myself to tap into the feelings of those I lead, I could better serve them. I could also harness the energy of their feelings to fuel our collective passion.

Empathy is often confused with *sympathy*, which means to feel sorry for someone in pain. However, empathy means being able to *feel* what that person is going through. And it often means reading between the lines to discern the truth behind someone's words.

It is a so-called "soft skill" or "people skill"– terms related to a person's Emotional Intelligence Quotient (EQ), which also include abilities like listening, communicating, conflict resolution, and cooperation. Hard skills, on the other hand, are capabilities that are technical or administrative in nature and much easier to measure than soft skills. These are related to our

Intelligence Quotient (IQ) and include managing a P&L, engineering, science, typing, computer programming, and accounting.

In the information age, among a sea of MBAs, empathy was often considered a nice-to-have skill. But as we reach the limits of what we can do with hard skills, soft skills are becoming a more and more valuable leadership commodity. In *Working with Emotional Intelligence*, author Daniel Goldman defines emotional intelligence as "the capacity for recognizing our own feelings and those of others, for motivating ourselves." Leaders must be able to get the most out of people in their organizations. But to get infinite outcomes, without wringing their teams dry, they must fully understand the hearts and minds of their followers. Emotionally-intelligent leaders, particularly those adept at empathy, know just how to do this.

Invoke Your Muse
Remember those moments when you realized that you knew what another person was feeling. Practice using this knowledge to persuade, connect to, or understand your subject.

Consider the following from "The Business Case for Emotional Intelligence" by Cary Chernis:

• A 1998 report from the General Accounting Office reported the increased effectiveness of Air Force recruiters when they began looking for certain emotionally-intelligent traits, including empathy, in potential hires. The Air Force found that recruits with these traits (of which empathy was second in priority) were more likely to succeed than those without them.

• L'Oreal sales agents selected based on certain emotional competencies significantly outperformed those selected the typical way – with a net increase in sales of $2.5 million and 63 percent fewer turnovers.

• Insurance sales agents in a national company who were weak in emotional competencies (including empathy) sold policies with an average premium of $54,000, compared to those with stronger competencies, who sold policies worth $114,000 on average.

Here are some tips from the Leadership Muse for developing this critical super-hero power:

STOP. When someone is addressing you, focus your attention on that person. Don't daydream, let your mind wander, or try to anticipate what you *think* a person is going to say. And don't check your e-mail. When you avoid the temptation to get distracted, your brain slows down and processes the words so that your Muse can transmit understanding. Understanding where a person is coming from, before you launch into your own agenda, makes you a more effective and inspiring leader.

LOOK AND LISTEN. This requires more than listening with your ears. It means looking at people. Examine their posture, body language, and facial expressions. Remember that the most honest and revealing communication in a face-to-face conversation is often non-verbal. Pay close attention to the eyes; if you listen closely to your Muse's inspiration and guidance, she will help you see into the windows of another person's soul.

CARE. John C. Maxwell says, "People don't care how much you know until they know how much you care." In order to fully practice the superpower of empathy, you have to care, *genuinely*, for people. You can't fake this and shouldn't try. People – especially empathic people – can spot inauthenticity a mile away. This means giving people sincere recognition, asking questions about their hobbies, lives, or families, and showing that you are truly interested in what they have to say. The Muse will help you listen to their answers and hear the truth about who they really are.

Empathy pays back. For L'Oreal, it translated to increased sales; for NASA, it saved lives.

CHAPTER 34

After a catastrophic electrical-systems failure on Apollo 13, Flight Director Eugene Kranz and his team at Mission Control had to perform the impossible. Fear and dread seized the team as they realized the gravity of the situation. "This horror that grips you becomes almost unimaginable in your ability to live with it," Kranz recalls. "But that is our job, to live with the risk. This is the nature of people who hold lives in their hands."

Kranz could sense the unspoken fear and pessimism in Mission Control. And he knew that he had to renew his team's spirit of optimism and creative problem solving in order to save the stranded astronauts. Insisting that they focus on solving the problem and not just on what wasn't working, he exemplified faith and optimism, inspiring the team to keep a positive frame of mind and completely banishing the dread.

During the crisis, Kranz' team was single-minded. Each person shared the same goal – to return the crew to safety. In the end, it was a successful collaboration of engineers, astronauts (both in space and on Earth), and technicians that performed successfully what everyone believed to be unfeasible. Kranz was innovative, composed, and empathetic. And his emotionally-intelligent leadership of a team of heroes made the impossible inevitable.

Chapter 35

THE TELEPATH: FASTER THAN A SPEEDING BULLET

"No mortal can keep a secret. If his lips are silent, he chatters with his fingertips; betrayal oozes out of him at every pore."

SIGMUND FREUD

A telepath can understand what is in someone else's mind without hearing that person speak. I wasn't sure that this could actually happen, and having a scientific mindset, I acknowledged to myself that it would be pretty difficult to prove or disprove. Then it actually happened to me.

My telepathic powers first manifested during a tedious conference, for which the keynote speech was boring and scheduled at the same time as the season finale of *24*, when my tablemate and dear pal, Bob, introduced me to another colleague, a programmer named Chris.

During the obligatory exchange of business cards, Chris expressed his desire to meet with me in the future to discuss his capabilities. At this point, the presentation seemed more interesting than my new contact, so I began to listen. Soon after the speaker got into his groove, Chris graciously excused himself, saying that he needed to make a very important telephone call to California. I looked at him with an awareness that seemed to come from out of nowhere. "No, you're not," I said. "You are going to watch the season finale of *24* like I wish I could. And *please* don't tell me what happens! I'm recording it!"

Chris turned red with embarrassment and said, "My goodness, I'm busted!" Then he ran off. He came back an hour later and reported that the episode had been an exciting cliffhanger. Moreover, he couldn't believe that I figured him out, especially since we had only just met and exchanged a few words.

Bob said, "See? I told you about her."

Perhaps the reader who is not experienced at mind reading will be skeptical about how this super-power can exist in mere mortals. But it can and does. For one thing, you can discern a tremendous amount of information through body language. Poker players tend to be adept at this. For example, most experts know that an opponent who feigns disinterest, freezes like a statue, or leans forward usually has a strong hand, whereas those with a weak hand are prone to aggressive betting, slamming chips on the table, or staring.

Invoke Your Muse

Did the little voice in your head ever tell you something important that you needed to realize? Think of a time when you ignored that voice. What happened?

But that's poker. Here are some tips from the Leadership Muse for ordinary folks without chips:

- Open palms: subject is relaxed
- Rubbing the chin: subject is thinking hard
- Gazing to one side: subject is being deceptive

These indicators were what gave poor Chris away. I guessed that his open palms meant he was relaxed – too relaxed for someone needing to suddenly make a "very important" telephone call. Assuming that he was being untruthful about the call, I could deduce that he was rubbing his chin to figure out if he had time to stay for the speaker. He also struck me as being similar to the special agent who is the hero on *24*, a personality type I recognized from my days at the Bureau of Alcohol, Tobacco, and Firearms – extroverted, intuitive, logical, and analytical. Plus, he was blond and not especially tall, like Kiefer Sutherland, the show's star. Nope, I didn't need him to tell me he liked *24*. I could read his mind.

Thanks to my ability to process his telepathic indicators in less than a minute, he was busted. The Leadership Muse is always giving clues to the contents of someone else's mind; they manifest in chattering fingertips, furrowed eyebrows, or nervous giggles. When you begin to notice these gestures and learn how to interpret the subconscious emotions or thoughts behind them, you, too, can be telepathic.

Chapter 36

"I was in my thirteenth year when I heard a voice from God to help me govern my conduct. And the first time I was very much afraid."

JOAN OF ARC, FRENCH PATRIOT

Clairaudience and clairvoyance are the ability to hear and see things beyond normal human capabilities. Many sounds and images cannot be picked up by the ear or eye, but nevertheless are perceived as having reality. Artists see their masterpieces before the images have been transmitted to their canvases; writers put pen to paper to transcribe stories that are already alive in their hearts; great composers hear their symphonies before they can be transposed to music. Artistic inspiration, great novels, and compositions often seem to come to their creators as bolts of inspiration from out of the blue, supernatural gifts from the Muse.

Of course, artists (and mystics) are often regarded as half-crazy, subject to strange visions and hearing voices that turn their lives and work upside down. But oftentimes, they are simply touched by the divine madness of the Leadership Muse, who delivers startling insights that strike a person as uncanny, eerie, and impossible to ignore, though many of us disregard them. My first experience with *clairaudiency* was shocking. It had and required no reasonable explanation (at least not to me) and it proved its merits.

In graduate school, while working on my master's degree, I became pretty good friends with my study partner, Sam. He lived nearby and was very supportive of me during a difficult health issue, often giving me rides to and from school. We were taking a challenging class together, Differential Equations. It was always one of my favorite math classes, and I enjoyed having the opportunity to live and breathe it with someone I enjoyed being around. Though I believed that we were friends, Sam ended up violating my trust – and certain principles of integrity and ethics.

One night, while talking with him on the phone about a homework assignment, I heard his voice clearly and distinctly say to me, "I am the devil and I will ruin your life."

"Huh?" I said. "What did you say?"

He repeated the startling statement. I asked him a third time, and he said that he didn't say anything. But I *heard* the words – twice. I didn't forget them either.

Soon after, he asked me to help him cheat on a test. It would have turned out badly for me had we been caught. At best, I could have been expelled; at worst, I could have ended up with a black mark on my transcripts that followed me throughout my career. Thankfully, my Muse had already warned me about him. He called me his friend, but in the end, when I did not violate the university's ethics policy, he discarded me.

I suppose I could have written the message off, chalking it up to the radio, or sleep deprivation, or some kind of delusion. But I chose to believe my ears (and in my sanity). And I did the right thing. It bothered me so much that I spoke to a professor, who confirmed that my academic career would have been ruined had we been caught. Since I alerted him to the cheating, he changed the tests, and I subsequently became unimportant to my "friend." This voice, or premonition, gave me a vital warning. Of course, I have no proof to offer, but it happened.

Many years later, I received another message from extra-sensory sources, this time *clairvoyantly*. I saw myself in a cemetery. It was very, very cold, and I was extremely sad. I remember seeing snow-covered flowers at a gravesite, and then the image disappeared. I didn't know what it meant but I remembered hearing the voice in graduate school. I hadn't been crazy then and was pretty sure I wasn't crazy this time. Instead of freaking me out, this vision made me value and cherish my loved ones in a more pronounced way, knowing they could depart from this life at any time.

Invoke Your Muse
What are the grand challenges you face that require a hero-leader? What kind of superpowers do you need? What is that little voice telling you?

A few months later, I discovered the meaning of this vision. Though I was busy with a hectic travel and work schedule, I decided that my grandmother's 96th birthday was too important not to recognize. So I pulled together a family celebration, and we all had a good time. She died that night. I didn't remember my vision until I was walking away from her gravesite. Suddenly, I had a *déjà-vu* moment – like I'd been here before. Following the graveside service, I stared at my feet so that my strength and resolve could hide my tear-stained face and so I could keep from slipping in the snow. As I looked at flower petals peaking through the white crystals, I realized that I had seen this *exact* image before – in my vision.

Whether or not they rise to the paranormal level, we've all had experiences when a little voice in our heads told us what to do. Furthermore, history gives us examples of impossible leadership where "imaginary" voices – from the Muse, the universe, or the Holy Spirit – saved a country.

Soldier and mystic Joan of Arc was a poor, young, French girl whose clairvoyant and clairaudient talents changed her life and the history of France and England. When she was about 13 years old, she was racing with other boys and girls. Because of her athletic skills, she was easily the winner. As she was running, one of the other children told her that she was flying, that her feet were not touching the ground. She suddenly got a weird feeling, as if she didn't know where she was. Then she heard a young, male voice tell her to go home. Assuming it was her brother or a neighbor, she ran home. When she got there, she discovered that no one had sent for her, so she decided to return to her friends. Then she saw a bright light that looked like a shining cloud. The same voice told her, "Be a good girl and go to church, and go to save France."

Though she was poorly-educated, Joan displayed wisdom beyond her years. She became skilled with horses and was one of the best riders in France. A brave general, she fought even when wounded and exhausted. She was good to those she led and good to her enemies. She was faithful to God and loved praying alone. The voices and the visions gave a peasant girl the divine inspiration to do what was unfeasible – save a country. Of course, at age 19, she was burned at the stake by the English for heresy, but she is not the first hero to sacrifice herself for her cause (and thankfully, we don't burn "witches" here anymore).

Hero-leaders listen to the voices in their heads. They follow their hearts, souls, and spirits. And in doing so, they inspire themselves to inspire others – and to do the difficult things a hero is called upon to do.

Chapter 37

*"Just as the visible world is sustained by the invisible,
so too do the manifestations of man find nourishment
in the visions of our solitary dreamers."*

**WAYNE DYER, AUTHOR OF
THE POWER OF INTENTION**

Today's world is in tremendous need of hero-leaders who will challenge themselves to meet impossible obstacles, who are prepared and have enough energy to stay in the fight round after round, and who can take it on the chin and keep swinging – like the boxer Buster Douglas, who against the odds and in honor of his dead mother, defeated Mike Tyson in only 1 minute and 23 seconds, leaving the previously-undefeated "iron man" dazed and barely able to stand. Regardless of the odds, hero-leaders succeed when failure is not an option.

Consider the story of Rodger, who leads a large software-development group which creates applications to support the day-to-day business functions of its clients. When an F-5 tornado devastated parts of Alabama in April 2011, Rodger's world of extraordinary leadership in developing business software became ordinary and unimpressive. Setting aside the challenges of technology integration in a complex organization of 18,000 employees and leaving an oasis of diesel-generated electricity, he rolled up his sleeves to help people in Athens, Alabama. He worked with his church to serve hot sandwiches, cold water, encouragement, and prayer to people whose lives had been turned upside down, many of whom lost everything.

There, he met two ordinary ladies who lost all their wordly possessions in a few brief minutes. They were resilient and grateful to be alive. Inspired by these tenth muses, Rodger returned to his work as a technology leader with thoughts of not just the financial systems in his domain, but the programmers he led who lost loved ones and lost their homes. Thankful that everyone in his group had been accounted for, he sent them a heartfelt, stream-of-consciousness e-mail:

Both ladies were praising God and thankful for all their blessings. Talking about living out Philippians 4:11-13!!! My hope was to be a blessing and encouragement to others, and I left as the one blessed and encouraged!

We need hero-leaders like Rodger, who find inspiration amid rubble and broken glass.

History reminds us over and over about the need for heroes, and hero-leaders in particular. These are the souls who prevail against all odds and face the certainty of defeat or death to achieve the "impossible." They courageously overcome fear – and inspire others to do the same. They don't give up in the face of danger; they take risks when few others will; they believe in what they are doing; and they rarely ask for anything in return. They led soldiers during Operation Desert Storm; they led teams of medical technicians in Louis Armstrong International Airport in New Orleans after Hurricane Katrina; and they led teams of doomed firefighters after the terrorist attacks on 9/11.

Perhaps this talk of hero-leaders inspired by a Leadership Muse seems like a mirage. Maybe the desire for inspirational leaders who can leap the tall buildings of today's business challenges seems as elusive as an oasis of water in a barren desert. After all, heroes, super powers, and Muses are just myths, right? Maybe, but the myth of inspirational Muses who can transcend the inevitability of doom is universally shared and universally needed.

Myths continue to rise above the findings of science; they span religions – and centuries. This is because myths are powerful. In *Myths to Live By*, Joseph Campbell writes of Carl Jung's assertion that:

Myths are telling us in picture language of powers of the psyche to be recognized and integrated in our lives, powers that have been common to the human spirit forever, and which represent that wisdom of the species by which man has weathered the millenniums.

A society that keeps myths, or "public dreams," alive will thrive and be nourished by the richness of the human spirit. Perhaps the Muse gives us a private dream, where we stand tall with our hands on our waists and our chests stuck out with big letter "L" (for leader) on our breasts. The leader who recognizes his Muses (no matter what form they take) and listens to their inspiration will be able to do the impossible – and motivate followers to do likewise.

The Muse-inspired leader will raise her skill sets to the level of artistic mastery and will always be on the lookout for the Leadership Muse and the lightening strike of inspiration – when she is ordering pizza for her geeks, in the sky overhead, at the hairdresser, feeling a bit nuts, lying awake on sleepless nights, and even on vacation. Relaying my close encounters with the Leadership Muse helps me to see the divine majesty that flickers on the periphery and to recognize the splendor of the insight that dances around, just beyond my ability to focus. My discovery started with my beloved grandmother, Corona. But inspiration is everywhere, for all of us, if we just keep our eyes and ears vigilant.

You may doubt the existence of laurel-wearing goddesses who whisper into the ears of artists and leaders alike, but do not doubt what they represent – the inspiration that our world so desperately needs. Kryptonite of doubt will neutralize the hero-leader's ability to succeed. We need these believing dreamers to save our world.

I dare to dream and make this hopeful wish for readers of these words, believing they will come true as we all embark on epic journeys of leadership:

I pray that you ask for and find the inspiration of your Leadership Muse. I offer gratitude for the beauty, truth, and joy that she will bring when she enters your life. Shed the sanity of the possible and believe in the madness of the impossible, to boldly approach infinity, and to humbly expect little in return. And I implore you to love all those you serve and serve all those you love. May the sparks of your talents be ignited into a blazing superpower of passion and purpose. And above all, I hope that you use your powers only for good.

Now, what did I do with that cape?

acknowledgements
TO MY MUSES

A cornucopia is the magic horn of plenty which stores the fruits of one's labor. I believe that the secret of this magical vessel is expressing gratitude for what you receive. My cornucopia runneth over with the fruits of those who helped co-create The Leadership Muse:

Doug Cureton, who in the true sense of husbandry, took special care of his wife so that The Leadership Muse could flourish.

Harriette Dodson, my mother, whose love and freckles dot my life and adorn the palette of who I am.

Corona Dash, my grandmother and Muse, and the motivation for this book, who is resting in peace with the blessed assurance that she is an inspiration in my life.

Carl Dash, my grandfather and perhaps the first man I ever loved, who made me see the magic in me and others.

Lisa Watson, author, wife, mother, woman, and baby sister who makes her big sister proud.

Stephanie Crowell, whom destiny made my friend and love made my sister.

Tereda Frazier, the angel who flew into my life and gave me encouragement and support when I needed it most.

Leslee Johnson, my developmental editor, who helped me think and organize seeds of ideas into a harvest of words and thoughts.

Taylor Mallory Holland, who dotted my Is, crossed my Ts, and kept me on my Ps and Qs.

Misti Burmeister CEO of Inspirion, LLC, who built a community with me and The Leadership Muse in it.

Jennifer Tyson of LeftRight Collaborative, whose artistry in design helped bring The Leadership Muse to life.

Frederick and Katrina Cureton, the very best graphics artist in the world and his wife and Muse

Adam Greenstone, who proved that one can get legal counsel and inspiration at the same time.

David Marsh III, the baby brother I'm so glad I didn't smother in his crib (or I wouldn't have had enough material for *The Leadership Muse*).

Loreen DeKort, whom destiny made my sister and love made my friend.

David Miller, an oasis in the desert of life.

James Williams, who outed my superpowers.

Madeline Weiss, the consultant's consultant.

Marion Harris, the teacher's teacher.

Kerry Stevenson, who started all this on a bus in Orlando.

Deborah Diaz, who helped as always.

Efrain Fernandez, who is such a masterpiece.

Robert Bruce, the Papa for life.

Paul Olson, whose synchronicity knew me then and when.

Peggy Marshall, Neil Rodgers, Hugh Goodlett, Marilou Bova, Dr. C. K. Kumar, and Wallace Clark, who will never know how much they truly touched my life.

One of the keys to successful leadership is to live, eat, and breathe in a constant state of gratitude and spiritual abundance. I will live every day feeling grateful to have been touched by all of you and inspired to dutifully pen The Leadership Muse.

bibliography

Andrews, A. (2008). *Mastering the Seven Decisions That Determine Personal Success.* Thomas Nelson.

Andrews, T. (1996). *Animal-Speak: The Spiritual & Magical Powers of Creatures Great & Small.* Llewellyn Publication.

Ashcraft, C. & Blithe, S. (2009). "Women in IT: The Facts." National Center for Women and Information Technology.

Atsma, A. (2011). *The Theoi Project: Greek Mythology.* **<http://www.theoi.com/Ouranios/Kharites.html>**.

Baumgartner, J. (n.d.). *10 Creative Myths.* Retrieved 2011, from **<http://www.jpb.com/creative/article_creative_myths.php>**.

Beers, R. (2008). *Divine Moments for Leaders.* Tyndale House Publishers.

Bennis, W. (2009). *On Becoming a Leader.* Basic Books.

Beyer, K. (2009). *Grace Hopper and the Invention of the Information Age.*

Blymyer, G. (2000). *Hairdresser to the Stars.* Infinity Publishing.

Campbell, J. (1993). *Myths to Live By.* Penguin.

Caplan, J.; Dell, K.; Dorfman, A.; & Fitzpatrick, L. (n.d.). "Time's Best Inventions of 2008." Retrieved 2010, from **<http://www.time.com/time/specials/packages/ completelist/0,,1852747,00.html>**.

Casson, H. (1910). *History of the Telephone.* Pine Hill.

Chernis, C. (1999). "The Business Case for Emotional Intelligence." *Consortium for Research on Emotional Intelligence in Organizations.*

Collins, J. (2001). *Good to Great: Why Some Companies Make the Leap ... and Others Don't.* Harper Business.

Covey, S. (2009). *The 7 Habits of Highly Effective People.* Free Press.

Cramm, S. (2009). *8 Things We Hate About IT: Moving Beyond the Frustrations to Form a New Partnership with IT.* Harvard Business Press.

Croucher, R. (2003). "Give Me This Mountain." Retrieved December 2010, from **<http://jmm.aaa.net.au/articles/2376.htm>**.

Cummings, J. F. (2008). *How to Rule the World: Lessons in Conquest for the Modern Prince.* Blue Ocean Press.

Daft, R. (2007). *Organizational Theory and Design.* South-Western Cengage Learning.

Dix, A. (n.d.). "Silly Ideas." Retrieved June 26, 2011, from Research and Innovation Techniques: **<http://www.comp.lancs.ac.uk/~dixa/resmeth/away-day/group-ideas.html>**.

Dyer, W. (2005). *The Power of Intention.* Hay House.

Estrin, J. (2008). *Closing the Innovation Gap: Reigniting the Spark of Creativity in a Global Economy.* McGraw-Hill.

Frankl, V. (1959). *Man's Search for Meaning.* Beacon Press.

Friedman, T. (2000). *The Lexus and the Olive Tree: Understanding Globalization.* Anchor.

Gerstner, L. V. (2002). *Who Says Elephants Can't Dance? Inside IBM's Historic Turnaround.* Collins.

Ghaemi, N. (2011). *A First-Rate Madness: Uncovering the Links Between Leadership and Mental Illness.* Penguin Press HC.

Glen, P. (2002). *Leading Geeks: How to Manage and Lead People Who Deliver Technology.* Jossey-Bass.

Goldman, D. (2000). *Working with Emotional Intelligence.* Bantam.

Graham, C. (n.d.). *More Money, Less Mirth.*

Greenleaf, R. (2002). *Servant Leadership: A Journey into the Nature of Legitimate Power and Greatness 25th Anniversary Edition.* Paulist.

Hesiod. (2009). *The Theogeny.* (H. G. Evelyn-White, Trans.) digireads.com Publishing.

Hill, N. (2009). *Think and Grow Rich.* White Dog Publishing.

Hunt, A., & Thomas, D. (2001). "The Art in Computer Programming."

Irving, D. (Director). (1987). *The Emperor's New Clothes* [Motion Picture].

Lehrer, J. (2010, December 10). "Are Heroes Born, Or Can They Be Made?" *Wall Street Journal.*

Leslie, J. (2009). *The Leadership Gap: What You Need and Don't Have When it Comes to Leadership Talent.* Center for Creative Leadership.

Losey, M. B. (2010). *The Secret History of Consciousness: Ancient Keys to Our Future Survival.* Weiser Books.

Maxwell, J. C. (2007). *The 21 Indispensible Qualities of a Leader: Becoming the Person that Others Will Want to Follow.* Thomas Nelson.

Maxwell, J. C. (2007). *The 21 Irrefutable Laws of Leadership: Follow Them and People Will Follow You.* Thomas Nelson.

Morrow, I. (1999, November). "Defining a New Type of Organizational Leadership: The Heroic Leader." *Pace University Lubin School of Business Faculty Working Papers, Paper 22* .

Nelson, T. (1997). *I Was Wrong: The Untold Story of the Shocking Journey from PTL Power to Prison and Beyond.* Thomas Nelson.

Neruda, P. (2000). *Selected Odes of Pablo Neruda (Latin American Literature and Culture).* University of California Press.

Plato. (2010). *Complete Dialogues of Plato (26 dialogues) Gorgias, Phaedo, The Republic, Symposium, Phaedrus & More.* (B. Jowett, Trans.). Coyote Canyon Press.

Plato. (2010). *Phaedrus* (Digital Edition ed.). Actonion Press.

"Playground Revitalizes Underprivileged Area." (1964, November). *Ebony Magazine , 20* (1), p. 192.

Rich, D. (1993). *Queen Bess: Daredevil Aviator.* Smithsonian Inst. Press.

Salwen, H. & Salwen, K. (2010). *The Power of Half.* Houghton Mifflin Harcourt.

Shakespeare, W. (2011). *Shakespeare's Sonnets.* Amazon Digital Services.

Sims, H. & Manz, C. (1995). *Company of Heroes: Unleashing the Power of Self-Leadership.* Wiley.

Sinek, S. (2009). *Start with Why: How Great Leaders Inspire Everyone to Take Action.* The Penguin Group.

Swift, J. *Gulliver's Travels.*

Uldrich, J. (2005). "Benjamin Franklin's Extraordinary Leadership." *Leader to Leader* (No. 38).

Useem, M. (1999). *The Leadership Moment: True Stories of Triumph and Disaster and Their Lessons for Us All.* Crown Business.

Vince Lombardi's Winning Ways. (2011). New Word City.

Williams, K. B. (2004). *Grace Hopper: Admiral of the Cyber Sea.* U.S. Naval Institute Press.

CPSIA information can be obtained at www.ICGtesting.com
Printed in the USA
BVOW021318240512

290917BV00006B/35/P